Kindergarten Skills

Table Of Contents

The student pages in this book have been specially prepared for reproduction on any standard copying machine.

Kelley Wingate products are available at fine educational supply stores throughout the U. S. and Canada.

Kindergarten Skills **CD-3703**   Printed in the United States Of America   ISBN 0-88724-421-1

Ready-To-Use Ideas and Activities

Learning the basic skills are children's building blocks for understanding more complex concepts. The stronger their foundation is in the basics, the easier they will be able to progress through harder tasks.

Remember as you read through the activities listed below, and as you go through this book, that all children learn at their own rate. Although repetition is important, it is critical to help children build self-esteem and self-confidence by helping them become successful learners.

If you are working with a child, at home, try to set up a quiet comfortable environment where you will work. Make it a special time to which you each look forward. Do only a few activities at a time. Try to end each session on a positive note, remember building self-esteem and confidence goes hand-in-hand with successful learning.

The back of this book has removable flash cards that will be great to use for basic skill and enrichment activities. Pull the flash cards out and either cut them apart or, if you have access to a paper cutter, use that to cut the flash cards apart.

The following are just a few ideas of ways you may want to use these flash cards;

Take the 26 capital letter flash cards. Have the children put them in alphabetical order. After you are done, sing the alphabet song.

Take the 26 lower case flash cards. See if the children can print them in alphabetical order matching the lower case letter to the correct upper case letter. Talk about the upper and lower case letters. Which ones look alike and which ones look different? What sound does each letter make?

Take the number flash cards. Have the children put them in numeric order from one to forty.

Take the number flash cards, use the numeric side. In a classroom setting, randomly give each child one number. Have the children line up in numerical order. At home give a child a group of numbers and see if the child can put them in order.

When you first do this activity, select a group of numbers that run sequentially, shuffle them up and give them out. As the children gain confidence, start picking random numbers that do not run sequentially.

Do the same activity to demonstrate skip counting. Try counting by two's and three's. You may want to try having the children arrange themselves by odd or even numbers randomly or sequentially.

There are flash cards which have the basic math signs on them for addition, subtraction, equal to, greater than comma, and less than. Show the children these signs and go over them. You can even use them to set up simple equations. For example: 5+3=8.

Take number flash cards which show a numerical representation as well as the ones which have the number word written on them see if the children can match the written number word with the corresponding numeral. Start out using only a few cards at a time. Gradually add more cards as the children become more proficient.

Take the color and shape flash cards. Take each (black & white) shape flash card one at a time, look at it, identify it, and talk about it. For example: talk about the circle flash card. Where else do you see circles around you everyday; coins, the sun, tires on cars, many knobs on T.V.'s and other electronic equipment, etc. The oval is not as common, but you do see it in an egg or in a picture of how the earth rotates around the sun. Can the children think of any other shapes? There are some other really interesting shapes like a rhombus (an equilateral parallelogram), a pentagon, an octagon, a parallelogram, or trapezoid.

Take the set of colored shape flash cards and the black and white ones and see if the children can match the black and white shape to the correct colored shape. This could be a great way to start a discussion on attributes. For example: we have two cards that have squares on them. They are alike in that both are squares. They are different in that one is brown and the other is not.

Place the set of colored shape flash cards face up on a table. Take the set of flash cards that have the name of each shape written on them and see if the children can match the shape word with the shape. See if the children can sound out the shape word.

Take the colored shape flash cards and see if the children can tell you what color each shape is. Talk about the colors. Where in their everyday life do they see these colors and what other colors do they see? Take the flash cards that have the color words written on them and have the children match the color word to the correct colored shape flash card.

Name _____

Follow the maze to get the bowling ball to the bowling pins.

4 **CD-3703**

Name_____
Follow the maze to help Fido find his way home.

Help Farmer Julie find her cow by following the maze.

Name _____
Follow the maze to help the puppy friends find each other.

     CD-3703

Name_____

Trace the dotted line from left to right to help each bee get to the flowers.

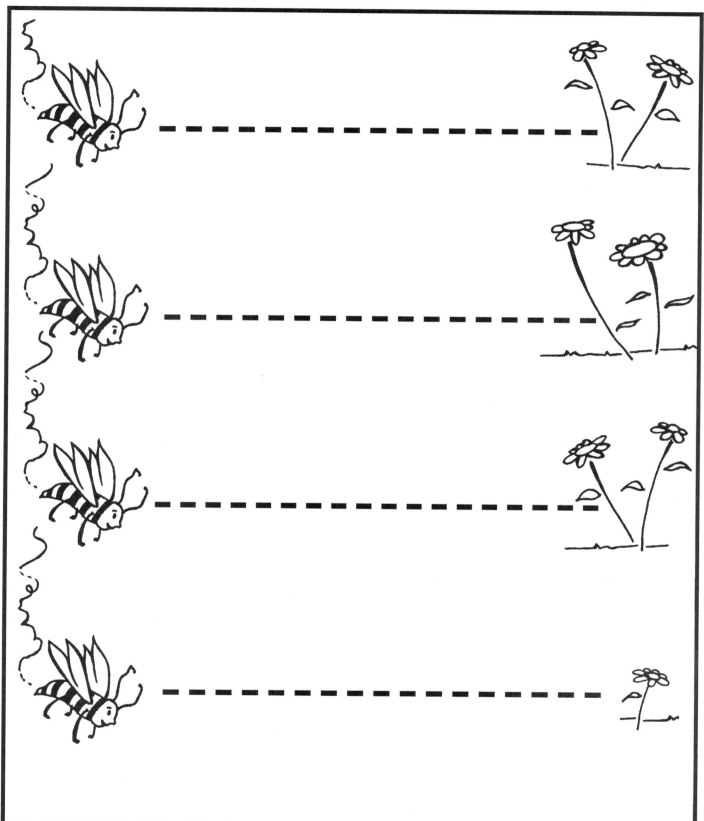

8   CD-3703

Name_____

Trace each dotted line from left to right to help each bus get to school.

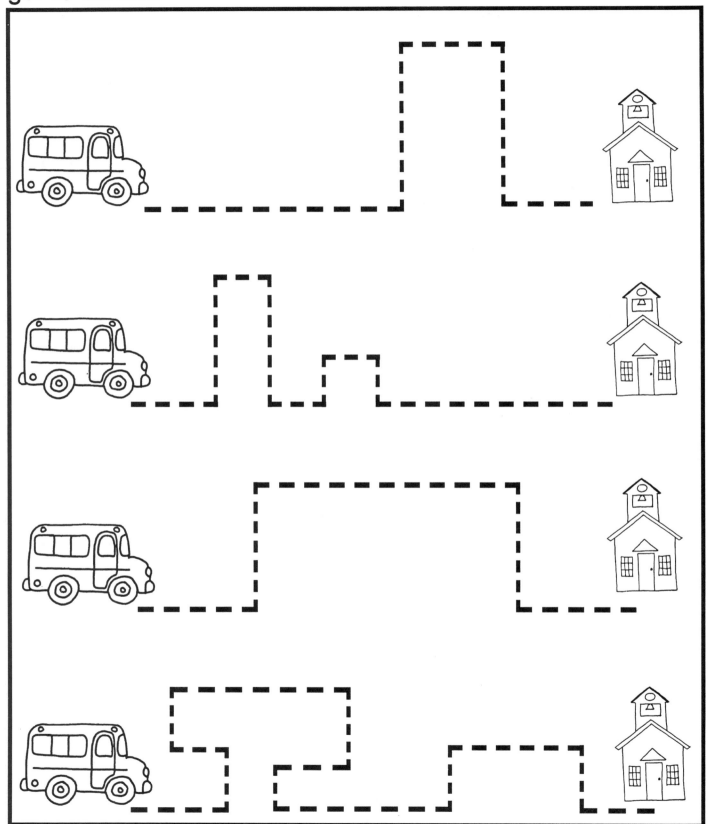

Name_____
Trace the dotted line to get the spider to his web.

10   CD-3703

Name _____

Follow the dotted line to help the girl find her way to the beach.

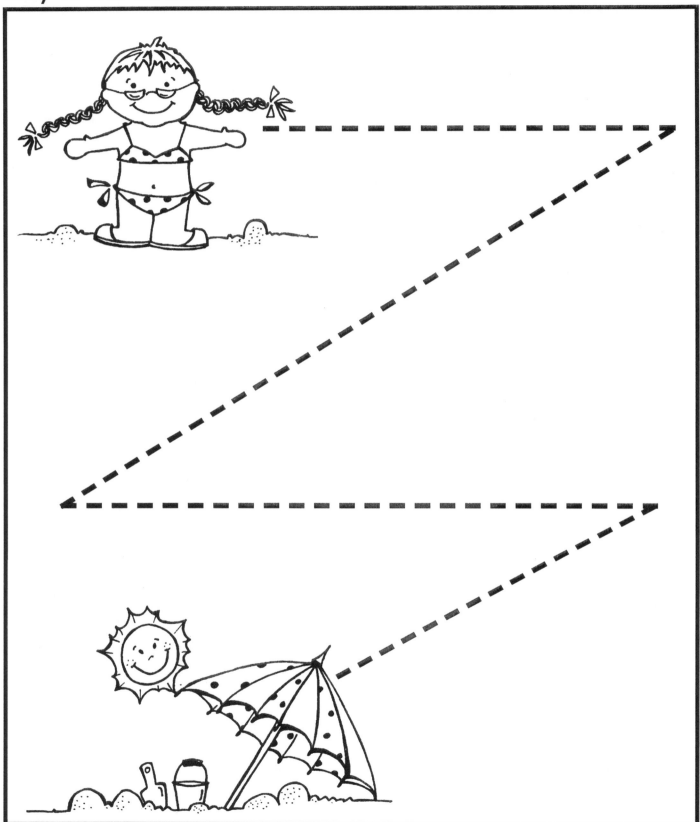

Name_____
Follow the dotted line and help the rocket get back to earth.

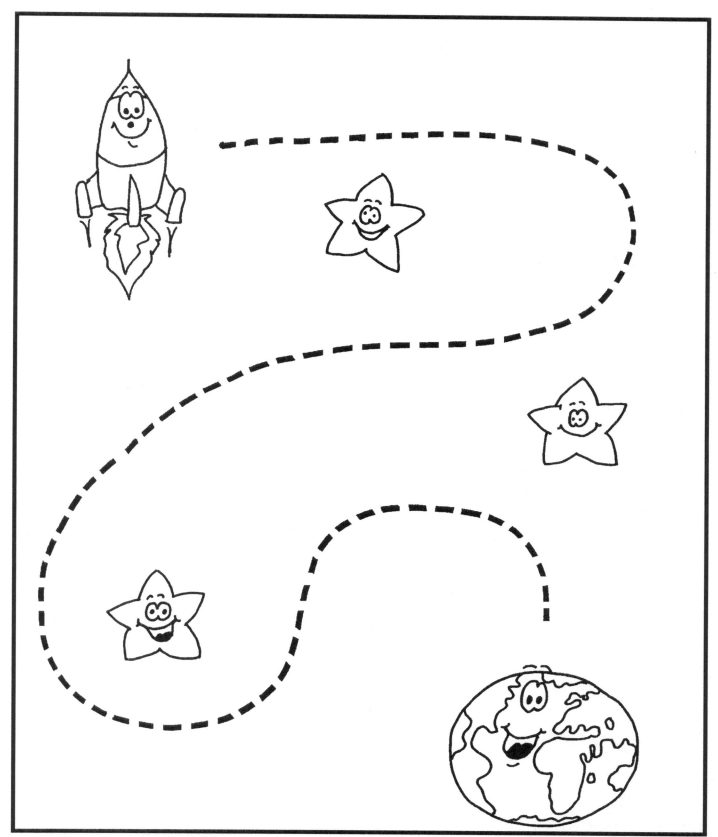

12 CD-3703

Trace the dotted line from left to right to help each frog hop to his lillypad.

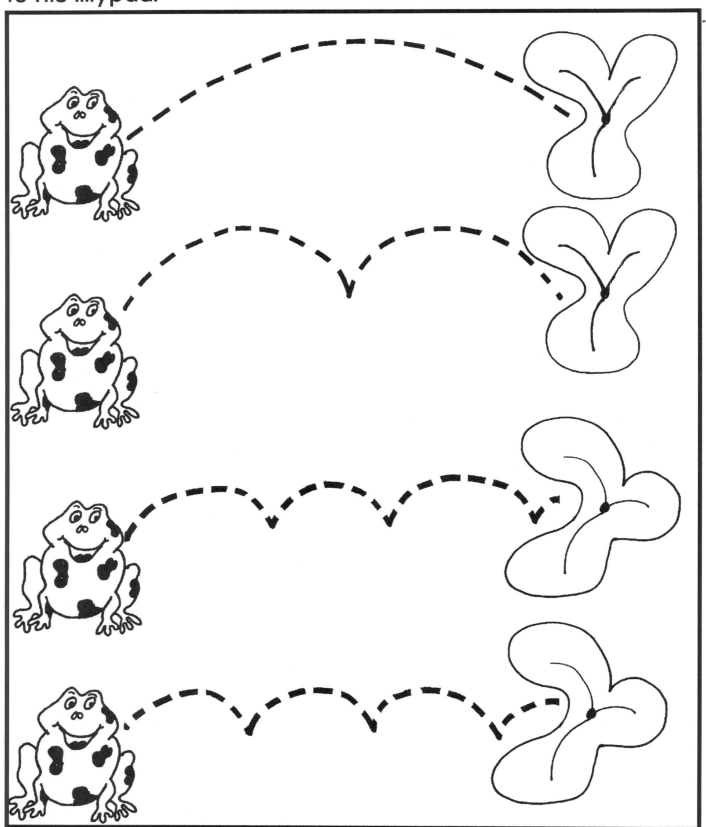

Name_____
Trace the dotted lines to get some water to each flower.

Name _____

Follow the dotted line to help the snail get to the flowers.

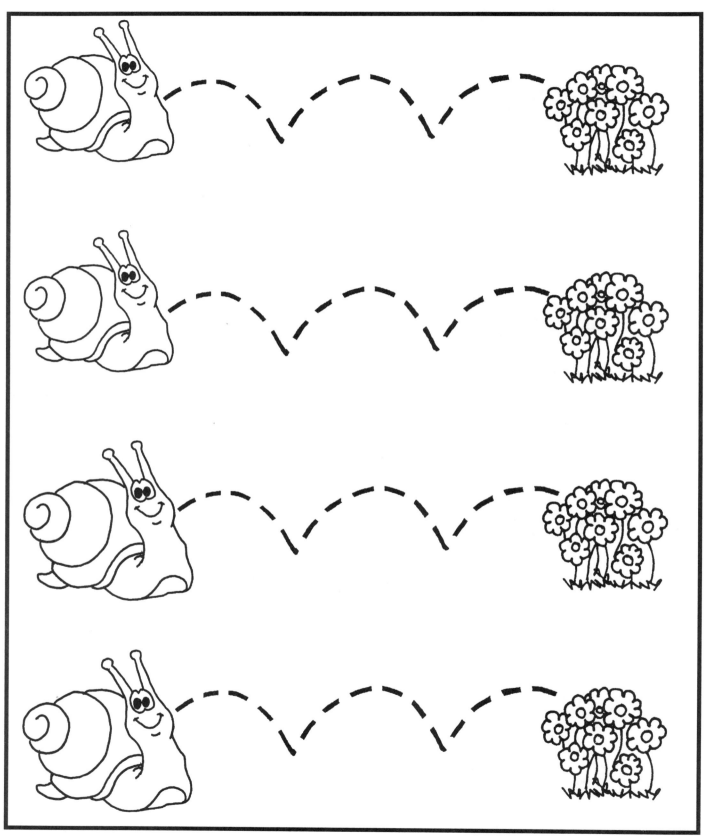

15   CD-3703

Name _____

Practice writing the letters.

Apple

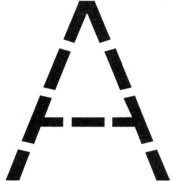

A A A

a a a

Banana

B B B

b b b

Name _____ Skill: Writing the letters C,c,D,d

Practice writing the letters.

Corn

C c

C C C

Duck

D d

D D D

d d d

Name _____

Practice writing the letters.

Eggs

E   e

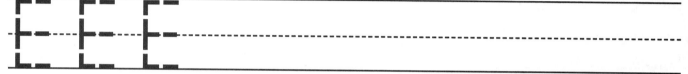

E   E   E   E

e   e   e

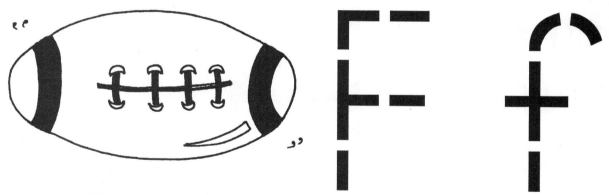

Football

F   f

F   F   F   F

f   f   f

Name _____

Practice writing the letters.

Garbage

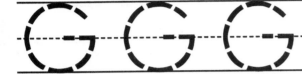

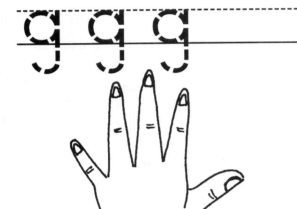

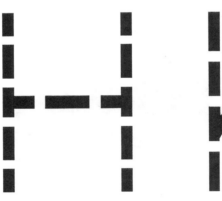

Hand

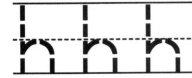

19   CD-3703

Name_____
Practice writing the letters.

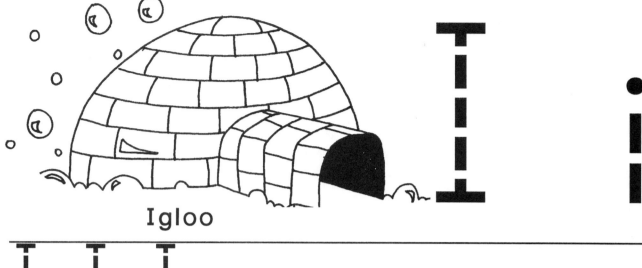

Igloo

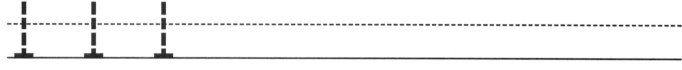

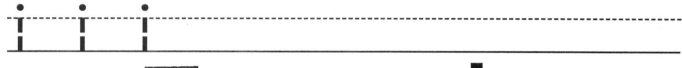

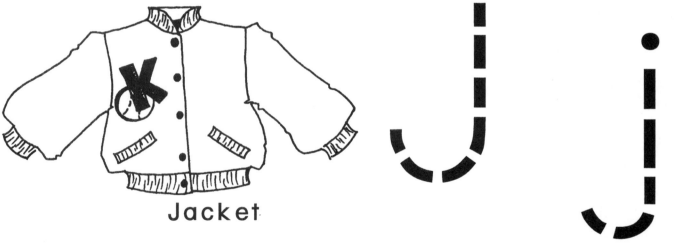

Jacket

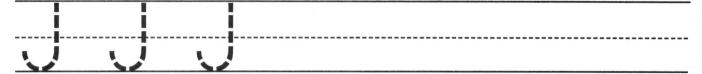

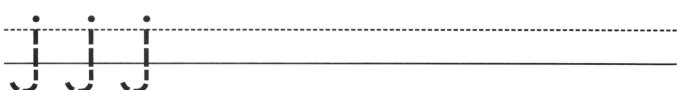

20   CD-3703

Practice writing the letters.

Keys

K k

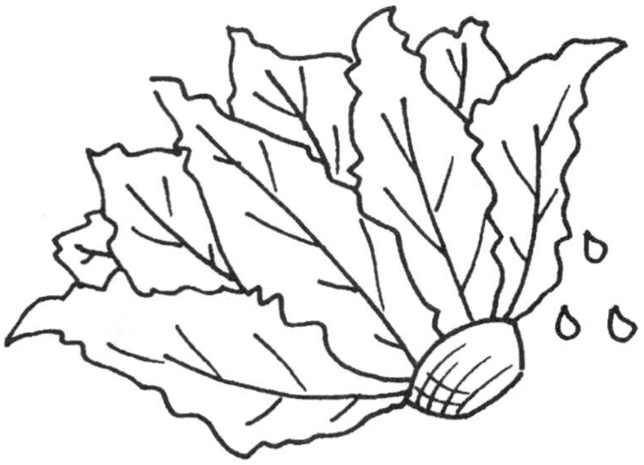

K K K

k k k

Lettuce

L l

L L L

l l l

Name ________________________________ Skill: Writing the letters M,m,N,n

Practice writing the letters.

M m

Mittens

M M M

N n

Needle

N N N

n n n

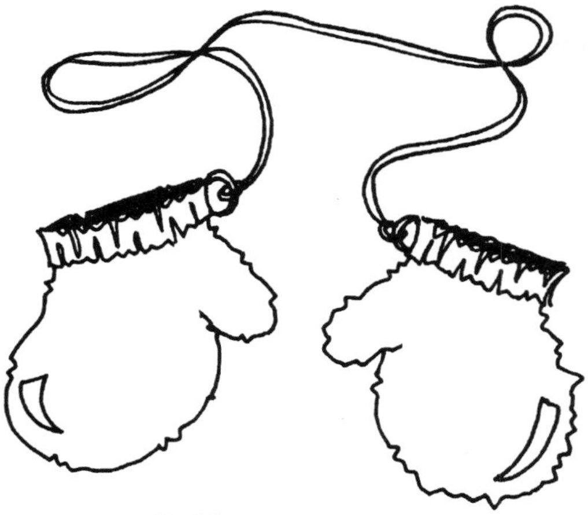

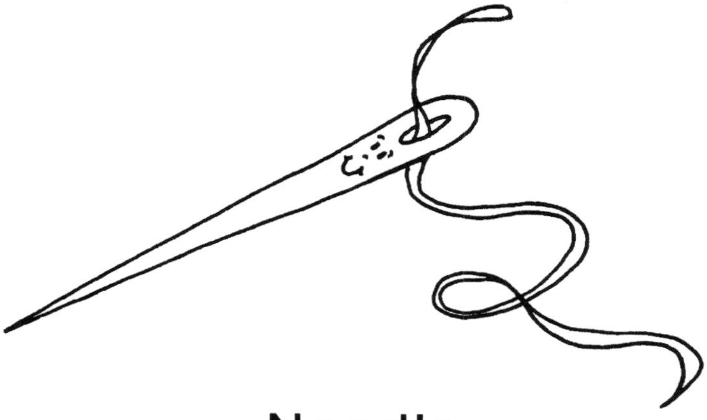

Name _____

Practice writing the letters.

Orange

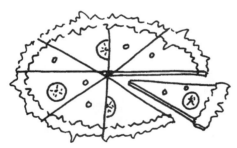

Pizza

P P P

p p p

Practice writing the letters.

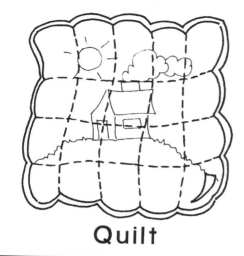

Quilt

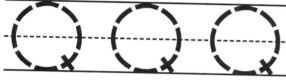

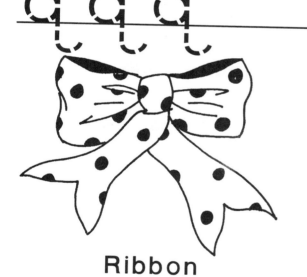

Ribbon

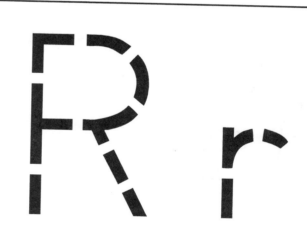

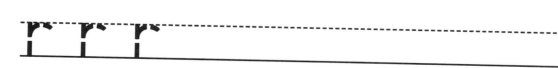

24

CD-3703

Name ______________________ Skill: Writing the letters S,s,T,t

Practice writing the letters.

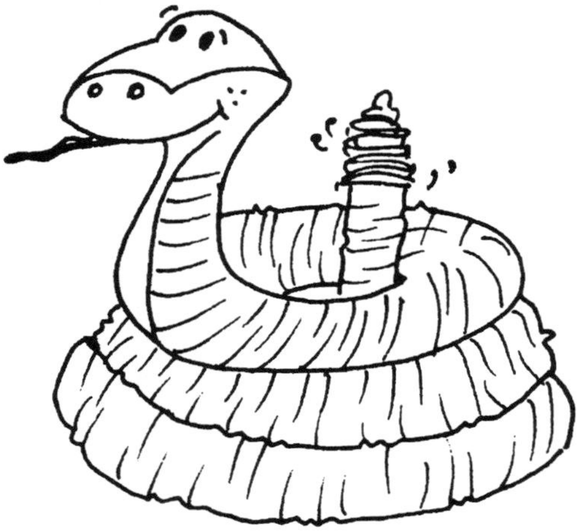

Snake

S s

S S S

s

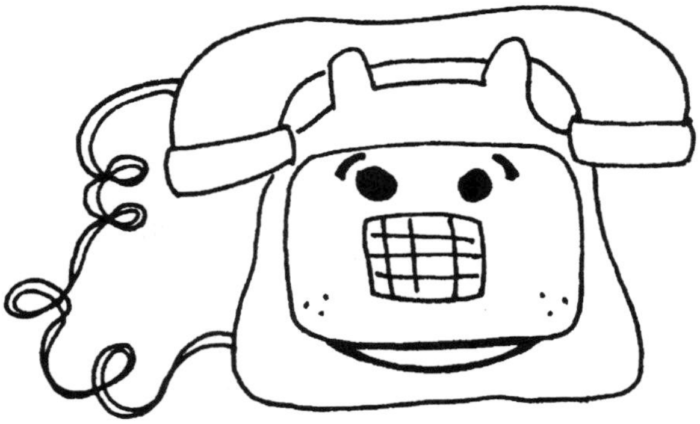

Telephone

T t

T T T

t t t

Skill: Writing the letters U,u,V,v

Practice writing the letters.

Umbrella

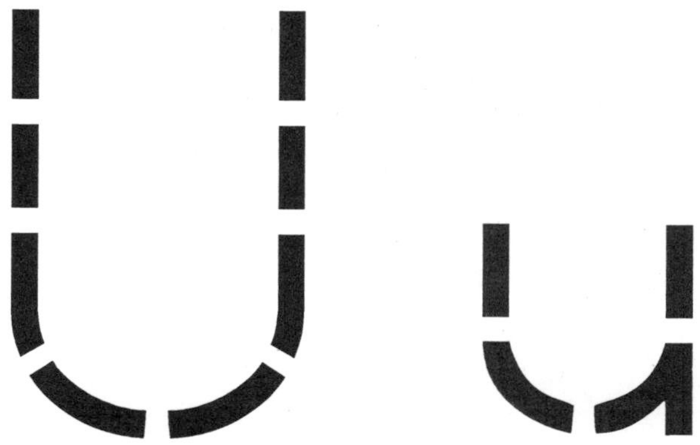

U   u

Vase

V   v

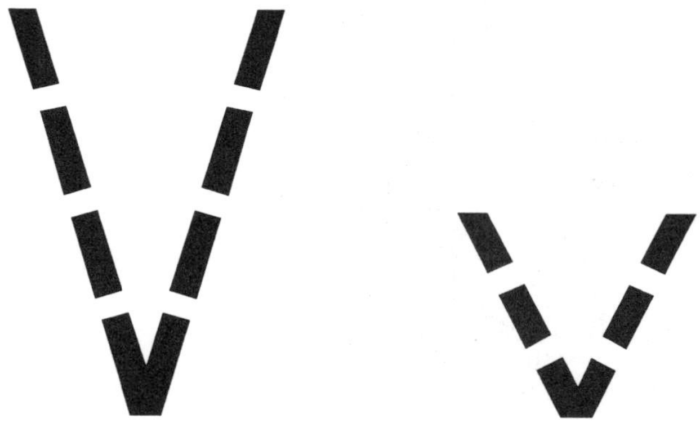

Name_____
Practice writing the letters.

Walrus

X-ray

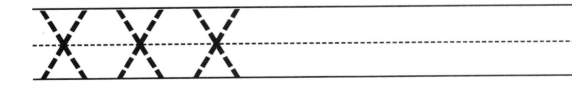

Practice writing the letters.

Yarn

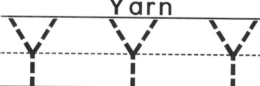

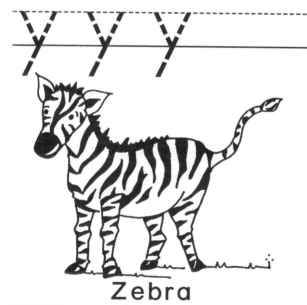

Zebra

Name _____ Skill: Writing upper case letters

Trace over the dotted lines to complete each letter.

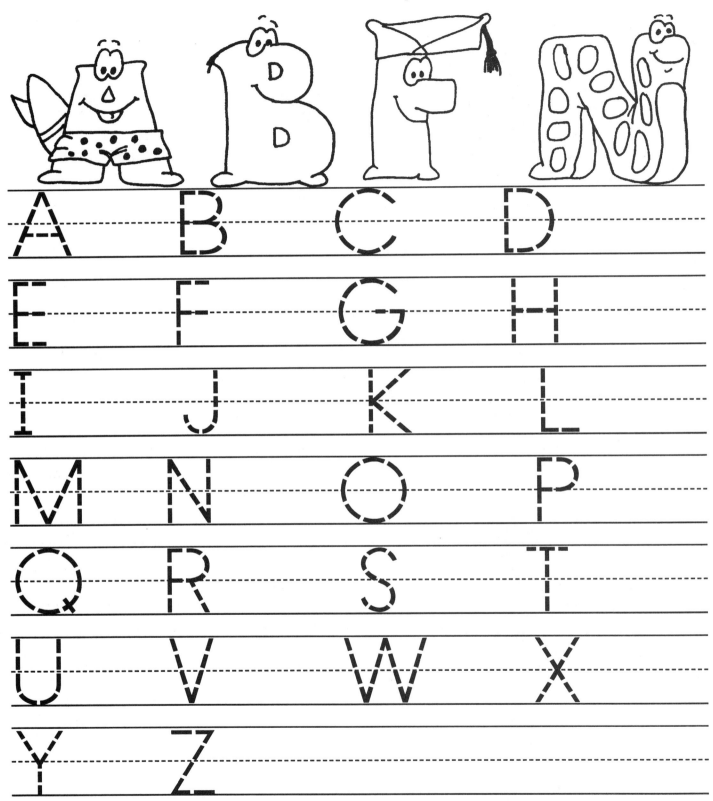

Name ______________________________ Skill: Writing lower case letters

Trace over the dotted lines to complete each letter.

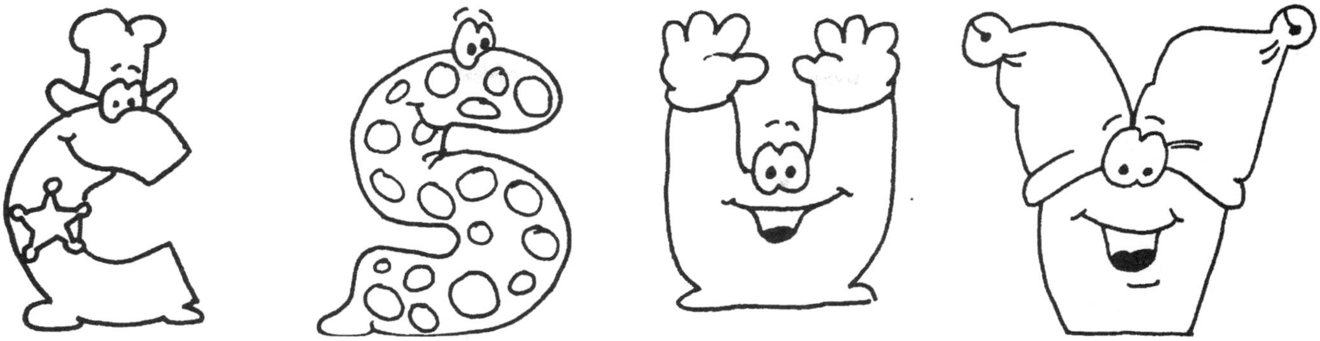

a b c d

e f g h

i j k l

m n o p

q r s t

u v w x

y z

Name _____

Connect the dots by following the A,B,C,s.

Connect the dots by following the A,B,C,s.

Connect the dots by following the a,b,c,s.

Name_____

Draw a line to match the pictures that are the same.
Color the matching pairs the same color.

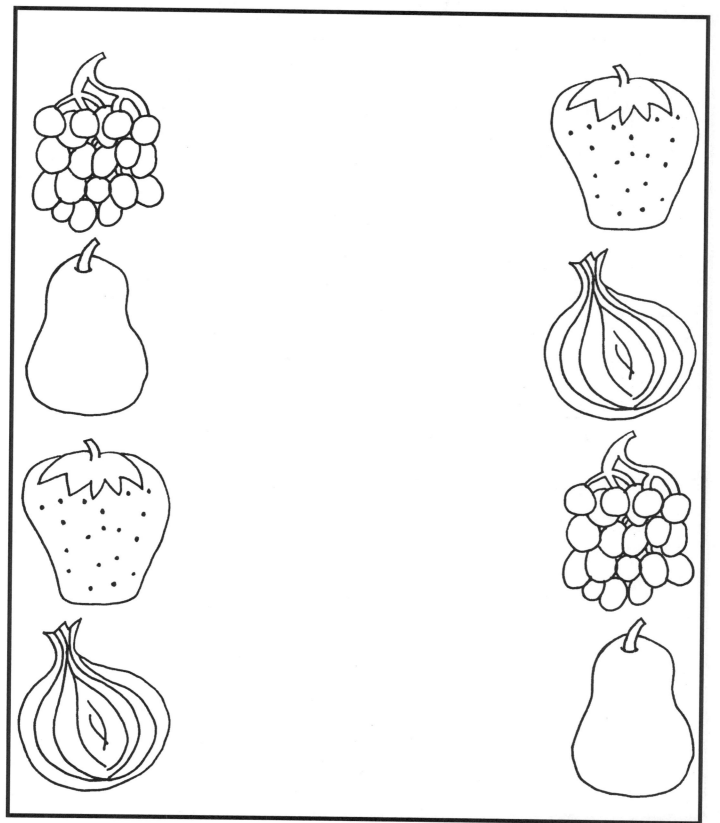

Skill: Recognizing
likeness and differences

Draw a line to match the pictures that are the same.
Color the matching pictures the same color.

Name _____

Circle and color the picture that is different in each row.

Name _____

Circle and color the picture that is different in each row.

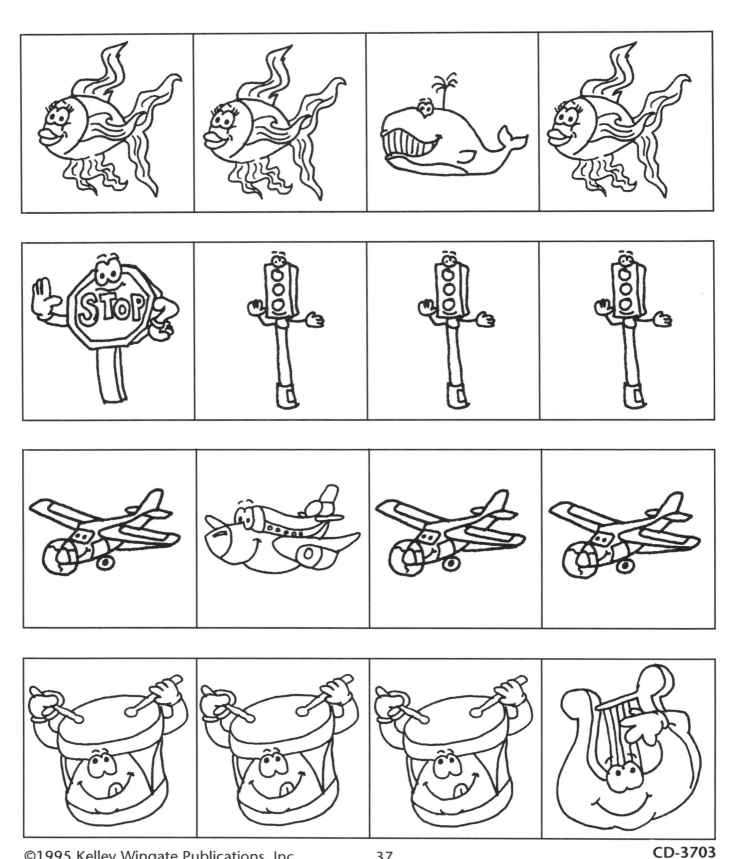

Name _____

Circle and color the pictures in each row that are the same as the first picture.

Circle and color the pictures in each row that are the same as the first picture.

CD-3703

Draw a circle around the pictures of food.
Color the other pictures your favorite color.

Name _____ Skill: Classifying

Draw a circle around the pictures of animals.
Color each animal a different color.

41   CD-3703

Skill: Classifying

Draw a circle around the pictures of flowers.
Color each flower a different color.

Name _____

Color the big ducks orange.
Color the small ducks yellow.

Name _____
Color the big balloons red. Color the small balloons blue.

44   CD-3703

Name _____ Skill: Recognizing big and small

Color the small presents yellow.
Color the big presents green.

Name_____

Color the long pencils brown. Color the short pencils blue.

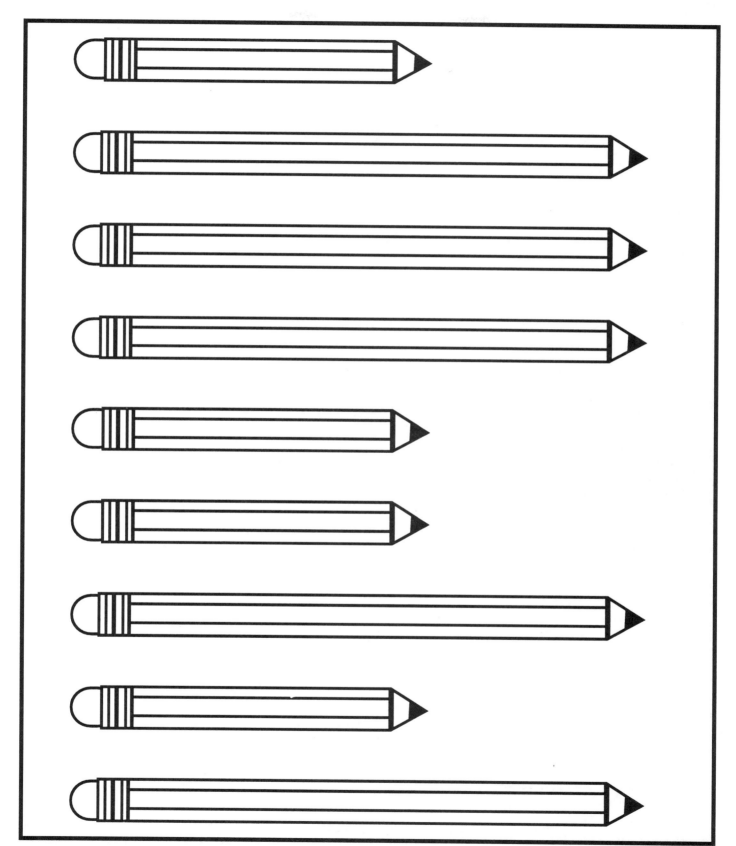

46

Color the short hot dogs orange. Color the long hot dogs green.

Color the long dogs red. Color the short dogs purple.

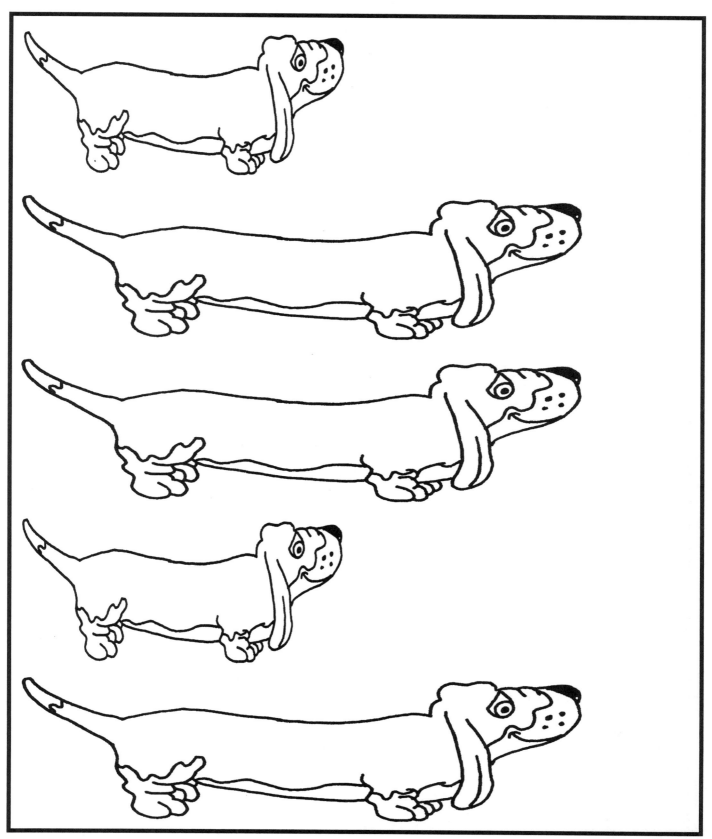

Name _____

Circle and color the largest object in each row.

Name_____

Circle and color the largest object in each row.

 CD-3703

Skill: Recognizing smallest

Circle and color the smallest object in each row.

51

CD-3703

Name _____

Circle and color the smallest object in each row.

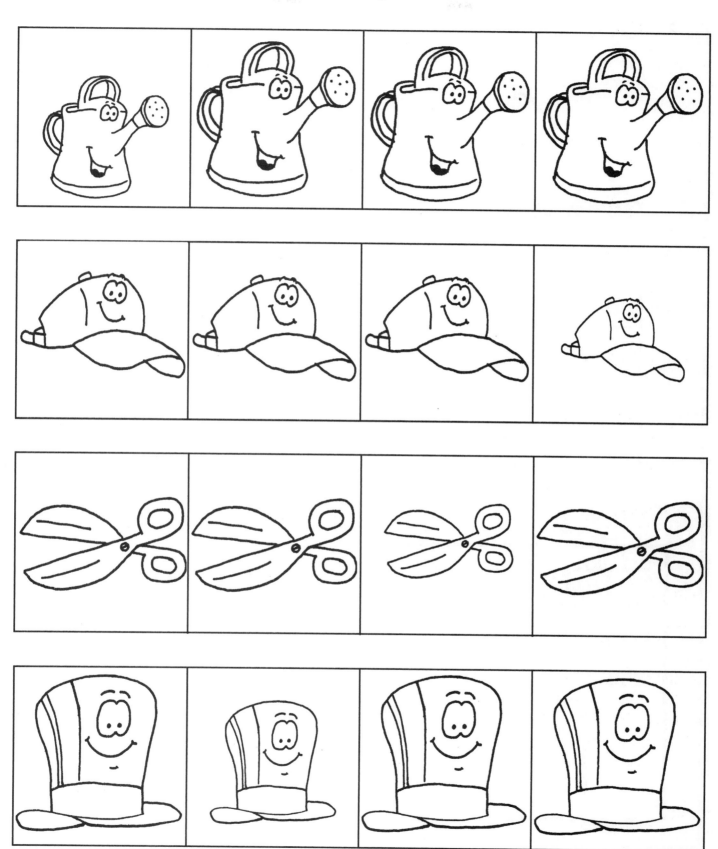

Name _____

✂ Cut out and paste the objects into the matching spaces to complete the picture.

Name_____

✂ Cut out and paste the objects into the matching spaces to complete the picture. Color the picture.

54   CD-3703

Name_____

✂ Cut out and paste the circles onto the correct flowers to complete the picture. Color the picture.

✂ Cut out and paste the squares onto the matching windows to complete the picture. Color the picture.

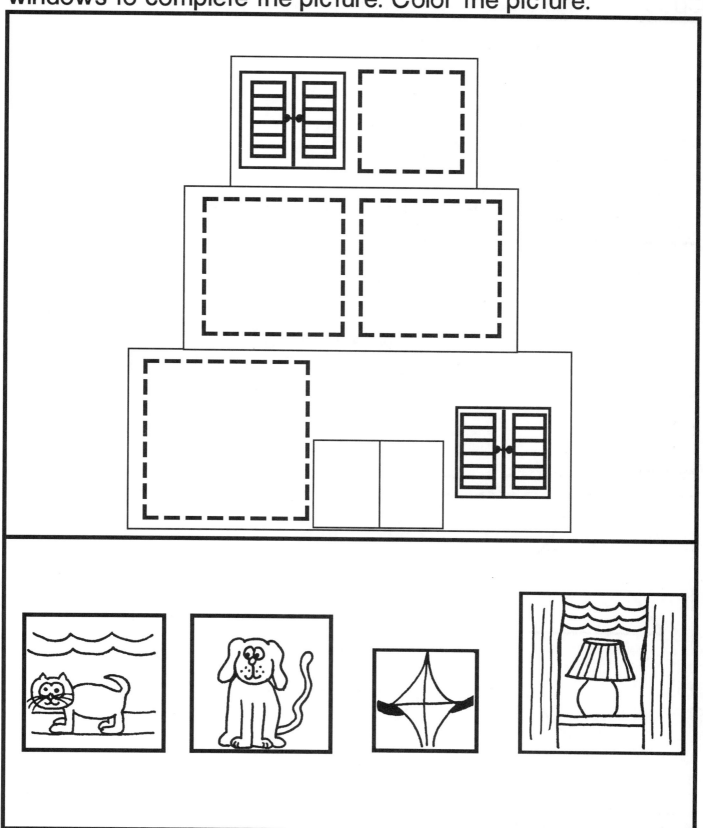

Name_____

✂ Cut out and paste the triangles onto the matching spaces.

Name_____

Color all of the circles yellow.
Color all of the other shapes orange.

Color all of the circles red.
Color all of the other shapes blue.

Name_____   Skill: Recognizing squares
Color all of the squares green.
Color all of the other shapes purple.

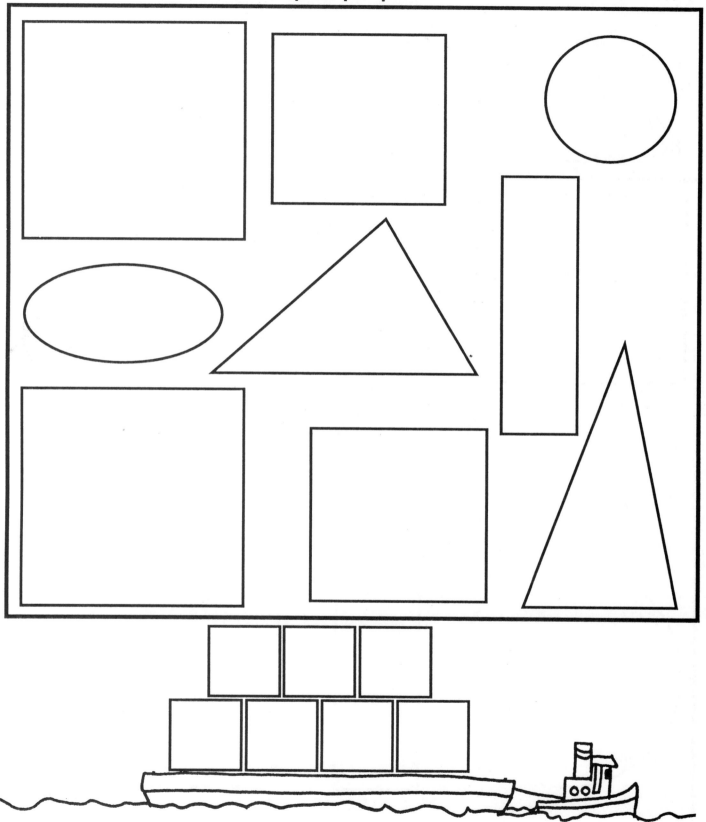

Name _____

Color all of the squares blue.

Color all of the other shapes yellow.

Skill: Recognizing squares

©1995 Kelley Wingate Publications, Inc.   61   CD-3703

Name_____

Color all of the triangles orange.
Color all of the other shapes red.

Name _____   Skill: Recognizing triangles

Color all of the triangles yellow.
Color all of the other shapes green.

Color all of the rectangles green.
Color all of the other shapes brown.

Name_____

Color all of the rectangles brown.
Color all of the other shapes pink.

Name_____

Trace the dotted lines to complete the squares.
Color each square a different color.

Name_____

Trace the dotted lines to complete the squares.
Color four squares green. Color four squares orange.

Name_____

Trace the dotted lines to complete the circles. Color three circles black. Color four circles red.

Name _____

Trace the dotted lines to complete the circles.

Name_____

Skill: Tracing triangles

Trace over the dotted lines to complete the triangles.
Make each triangle into a tee pee. Color each tee pee.

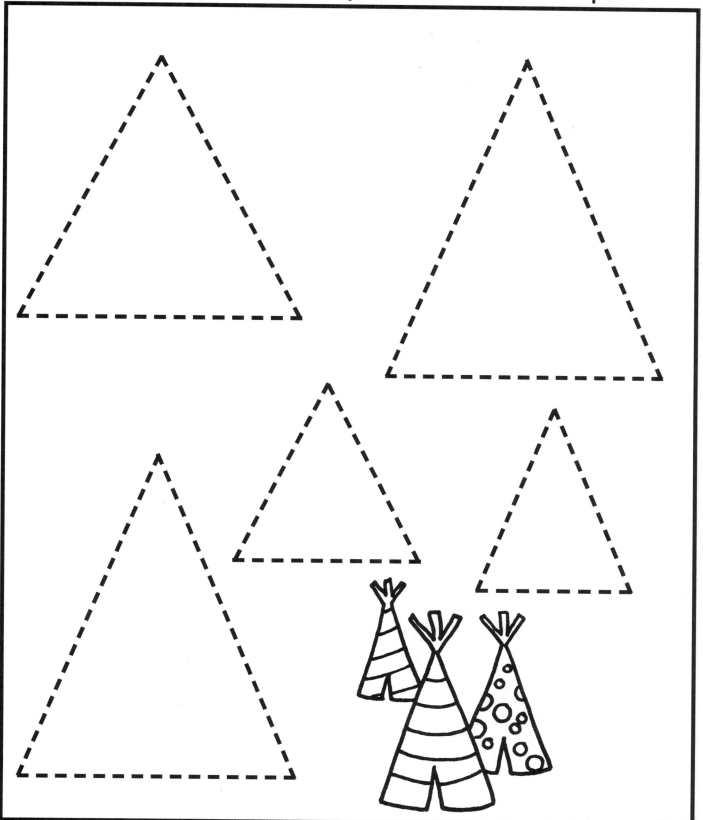

©1995 Kelley Wingate Publications, Inc.   70   CD-3703

Name _____

Trace over the dotted lines to complete the party hats.
Color each party hat a different color.

Name _____

Practice drawing each shape.

Name_____

Practice drawing each shape.

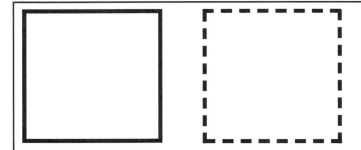

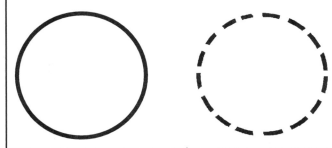

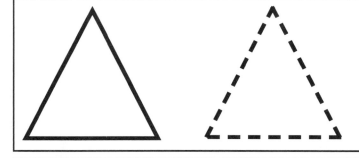

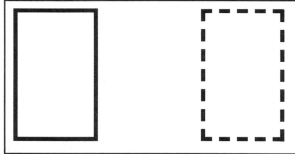

Name_____

Trace the dotted lines to complete the shapes.
Color the circles red. Color the rectangles blue.

Name_____

Trace the dotted lines to complete the shapes.
Color the triangles yellow. Color the squares green.

Name_____

Draw a line to match the signs that are the same.
Color the street signs.

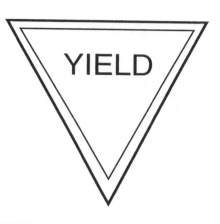

SPEED
LIMIT
55

WRONG
WAY

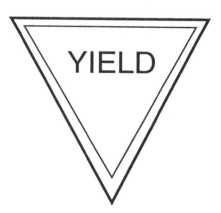

YIELD

WRONG
WAY

SPEED
LIMIT
55

Draw a line to match the shapes that are the same.

Skill: Reviewing shapes

Draw a line to match the shapes that are the same.
Color the matching shapes the same color.

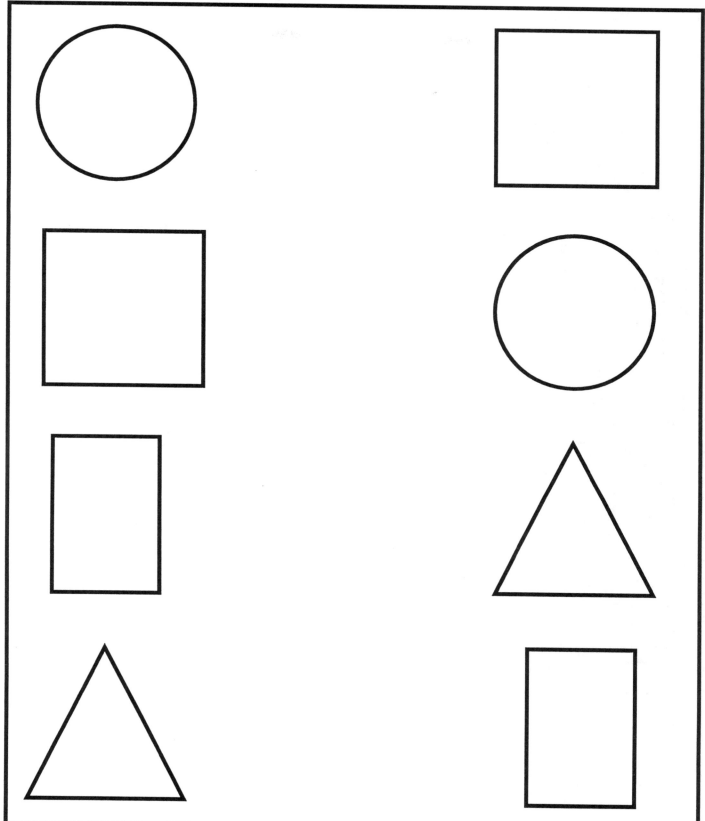

Name _____ Skill: Learning green and brown

Color each space with the correct color.

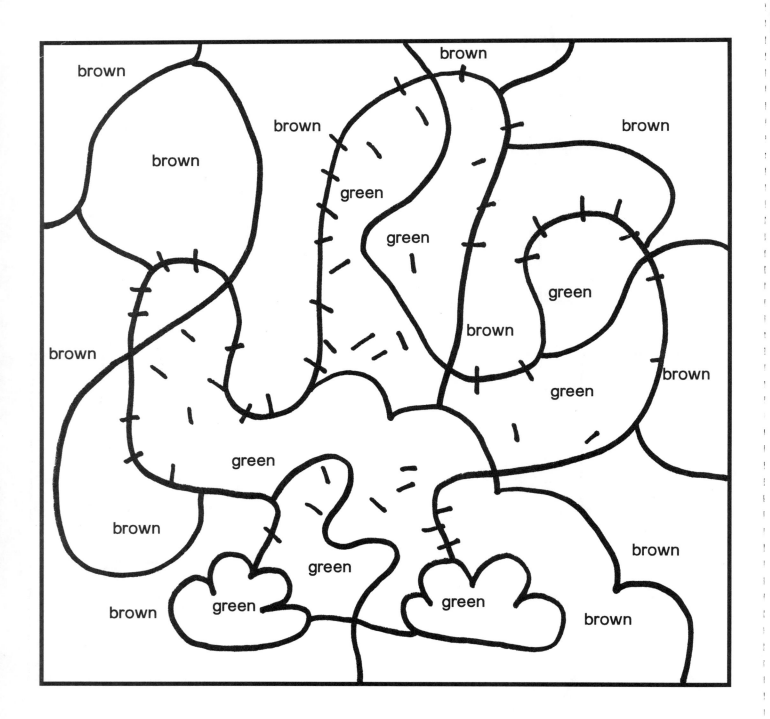

79   CD-3703

Name_____ Skill: Learning black and orange
Color each space with the correct color.

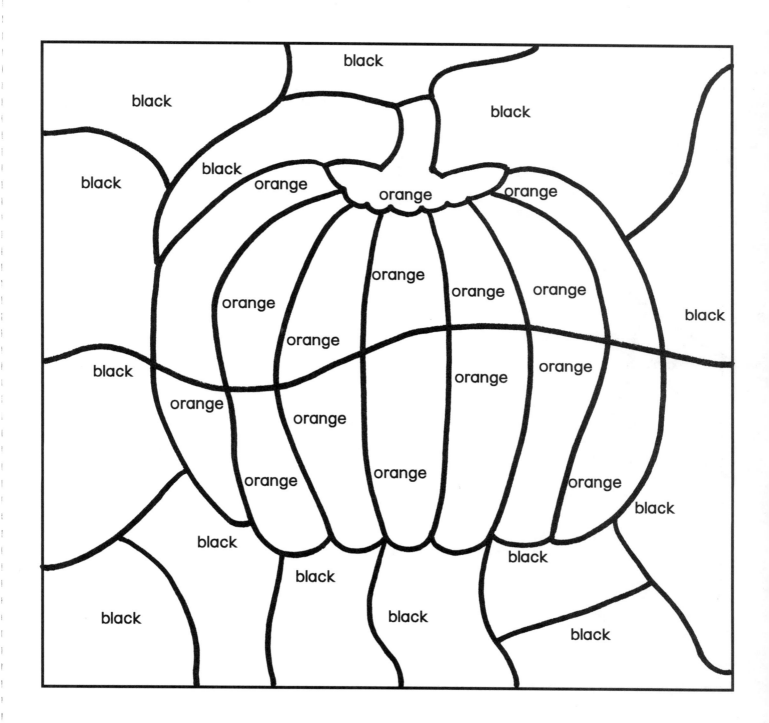

80 CD-3703

Color each space with the correct color.

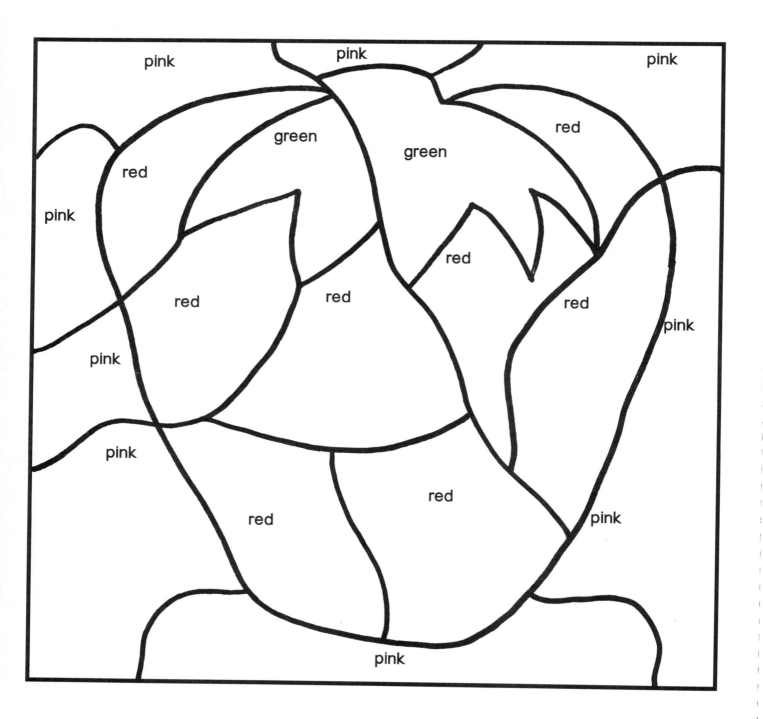

Name _____ Skill: Learning blue and yellow

Color each space with the correct color.

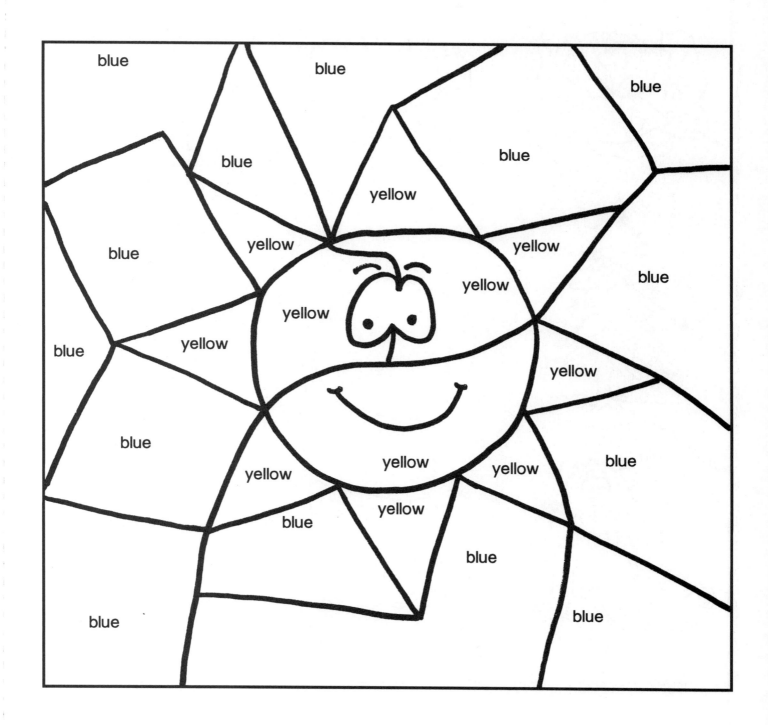

blue   blue   blue

blue   blue   blue

blue   yellow

blue   yellow   yellow

yellow   yellow   blue

blue   yellow

yellow   yellow   yellow

blue   yellow   blue

blue   yellow   yellow

blue   yellow   blue

blue   yellow   blue

blue   blue

82   CD-3703

Name_____

Use a green crayon to color the things that are usually green.

Name _____

Use a yellow crayon to color the things that are usually yellow.

CD-3703

Name _____
Use a red crayon to color the things that are usually red.

85   CD-3703

Name _____

Use an orange crayon to color the things that are usually orange.

CD-3703

Color each picture the correct color.

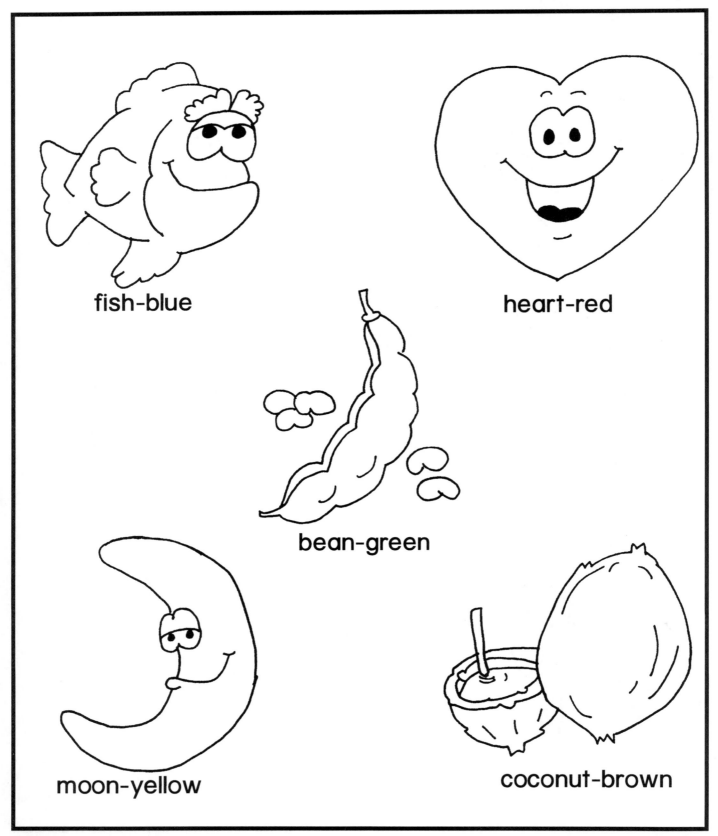

fish-blue

heart-red

bean-green

moon-yellow

coconut-brown

Color each picture the correct color.

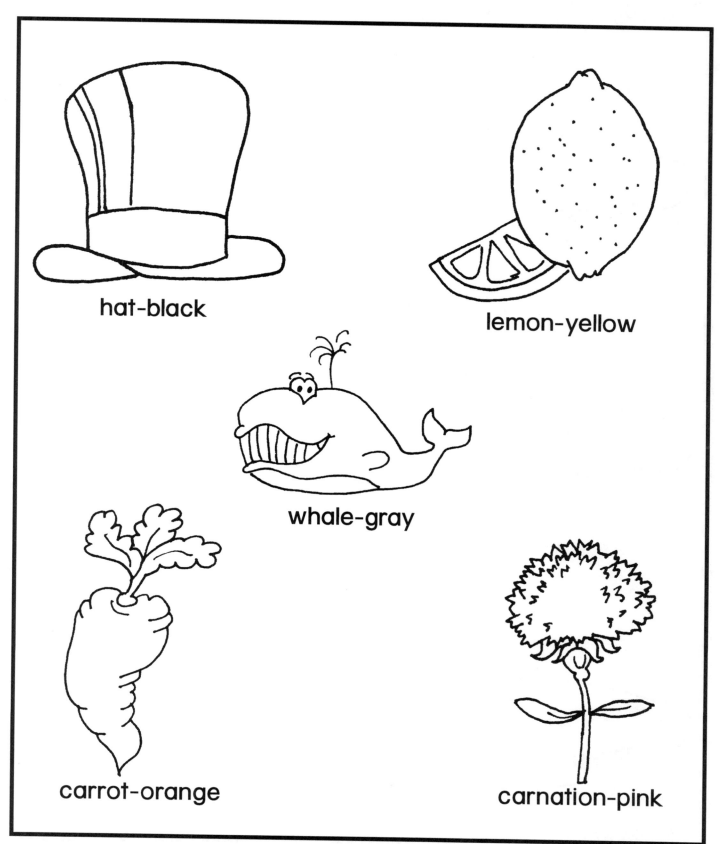

hat-black

lemon-yellow

whale-gray

carrot-orange

carnation-pink

Name _____

Color one shark green. Color one shark blue.
Color one shark red.

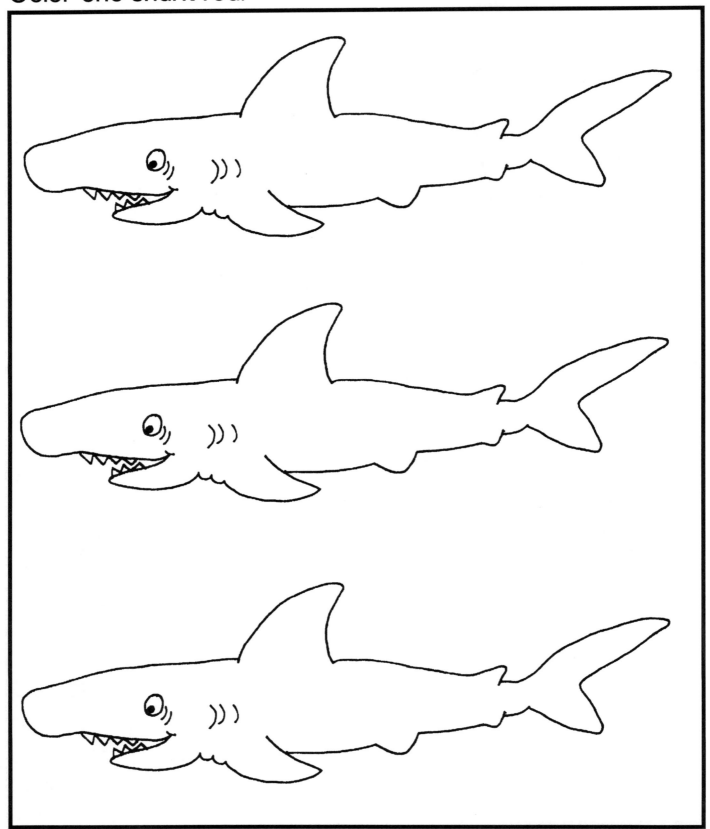

Name_____

Color two shirts purple. Color two shirts red.

Name _____

Color two bows orange. Color three bows yellow.

Name_____

Circle two objects in each group.

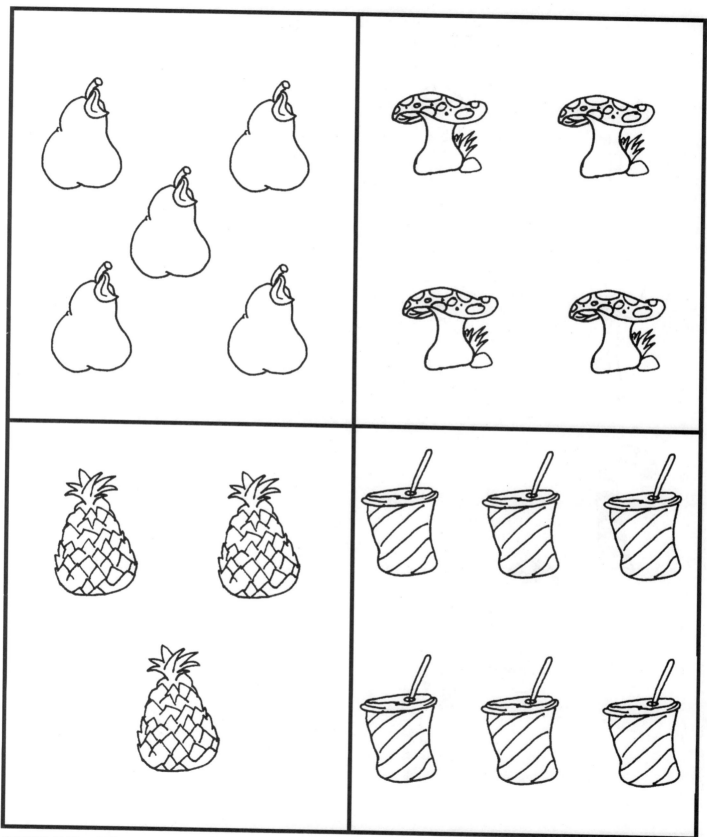

Name _____

Circle three objects in each group.

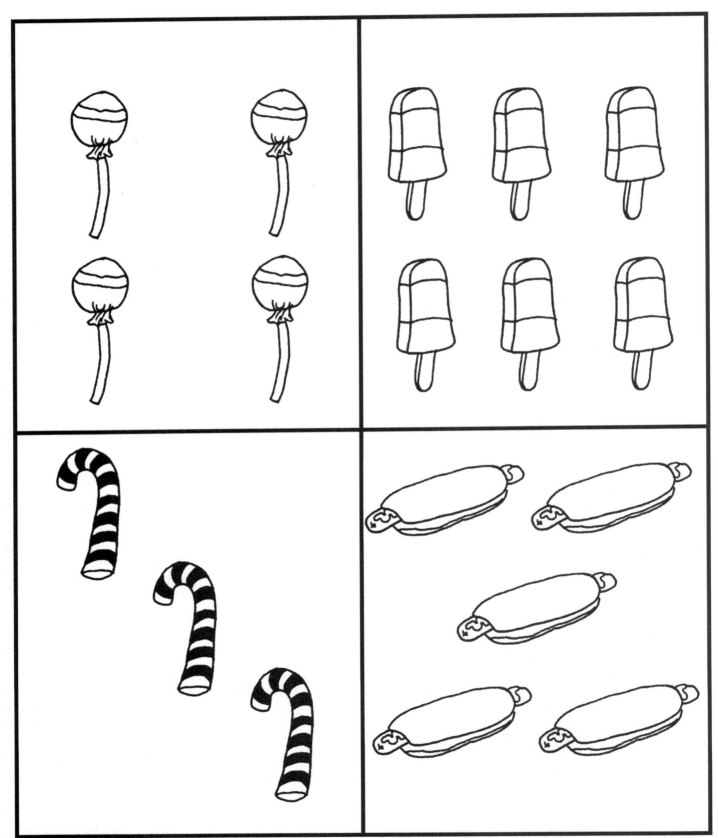

Name _____

Circle and color four objects in each group.

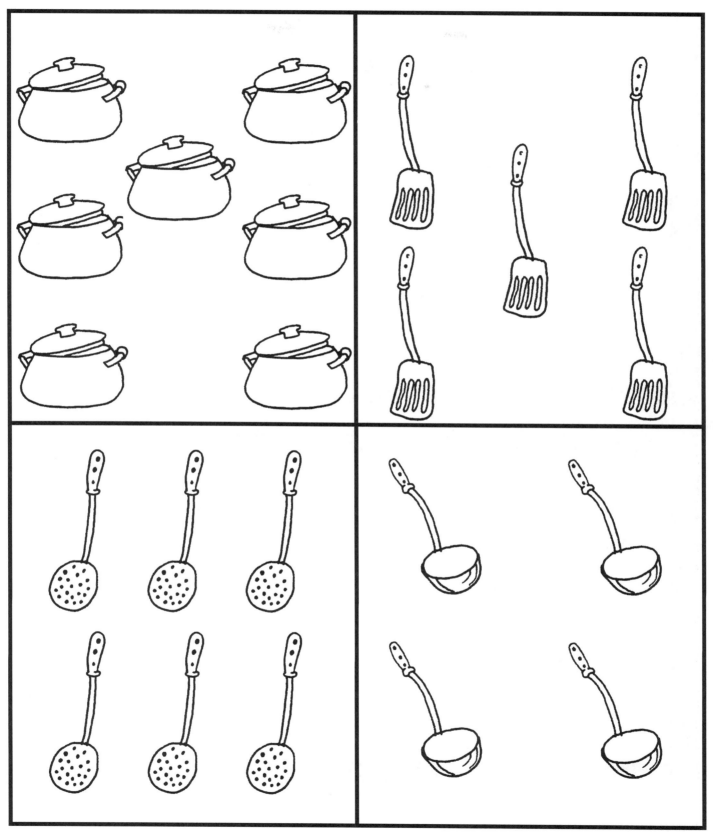

Draw two happy people in each picture frame.

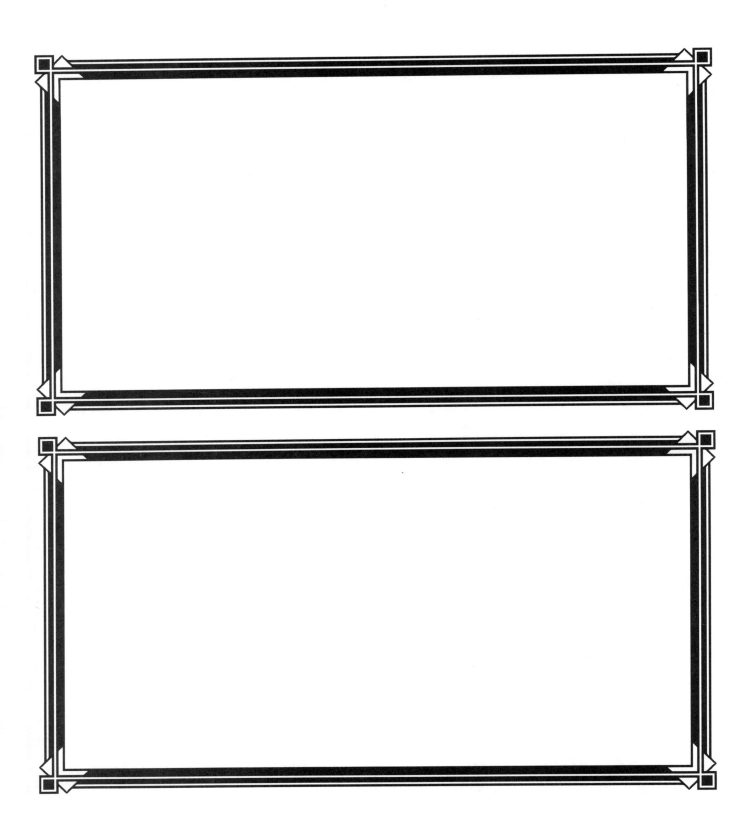

Name _____ Skill: Counting to three

Draw three nests in the tree. Draw two eggs in each nest.
Color the tree.

96   CD-3703

Draw and color four fish in the pond.

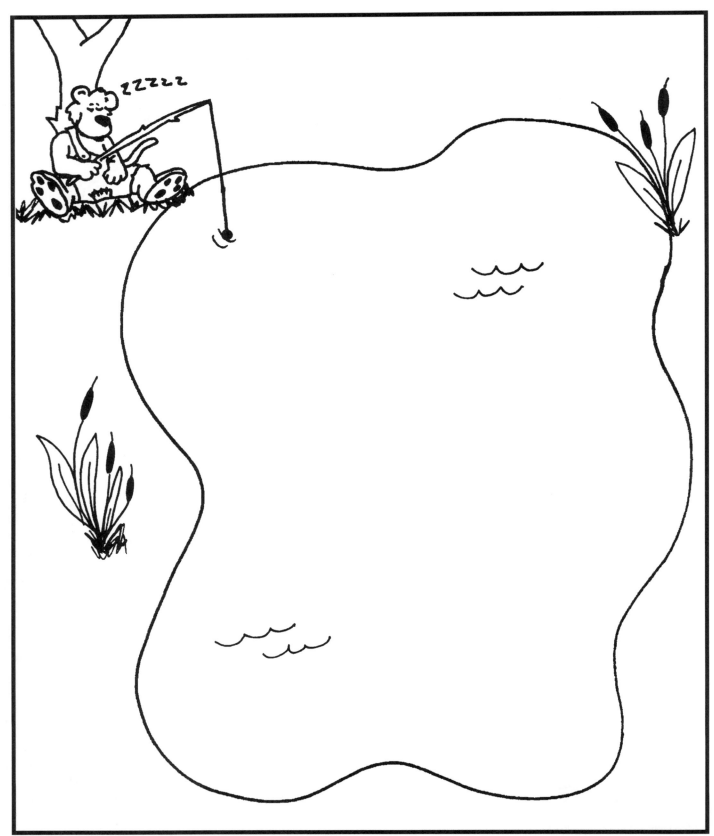

97 CD-3703

Draw five cookies on the plate.
Color the plate and the cookies.

Name _____

Connect the dots from 1-5 to find a delicious treat.
Color the completed picture.

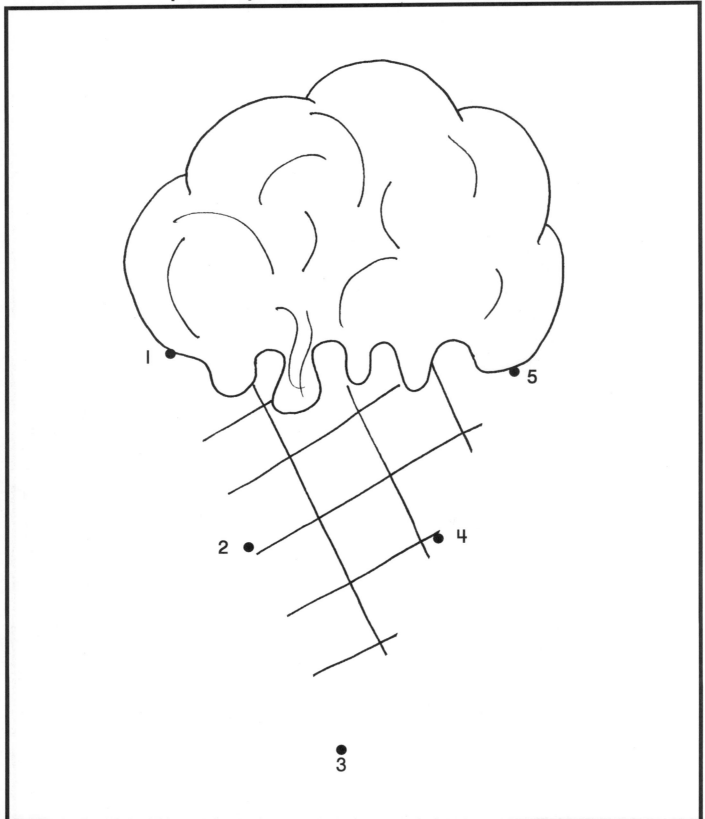

99   **CD-3703**

Name _____ Skill: Counting one to seven
Connect the dots from 1-7. Color the completed picture.

Name_____

Connect the dots from 1-15.
Color the completed picture.

Name_____

Count the number of objects in each row.
Circle the correct numeral.

     1   2   3   4   5

   1   2   3   4   5

    1   2   3   4   5

     1   2   3   4   5

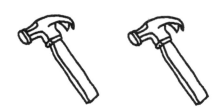   1   2   3   4   5

   1   2   3   4   5

       CD-3703

Name _____

Skill: Counting 1-6

Count the number of objects in each row.
Circle the correct numeral.

  1 2 3 4 5 6

 1 2 3 4 5 6

 1 2 3 4 5 6

 1 2 3 4 5 6

  1 2 3 4 5 6

     1 2 3 4 5 6

Name _____

In each row circle the thing that happened first.

In each row circle the thing that happened last.

Name_____

✂ Cut out the pictures below and paste in order from first to last.

1	2
3	4

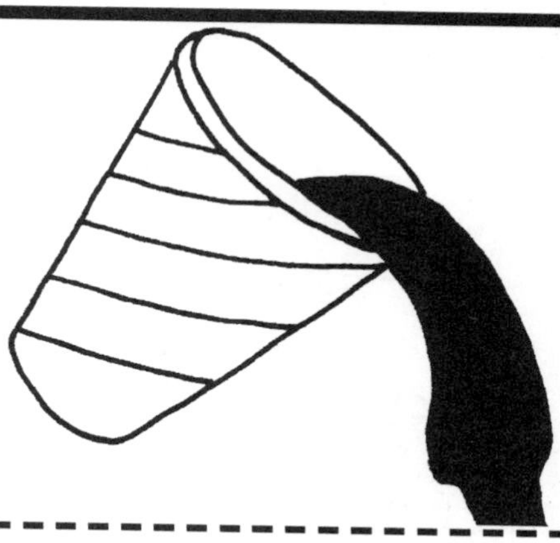

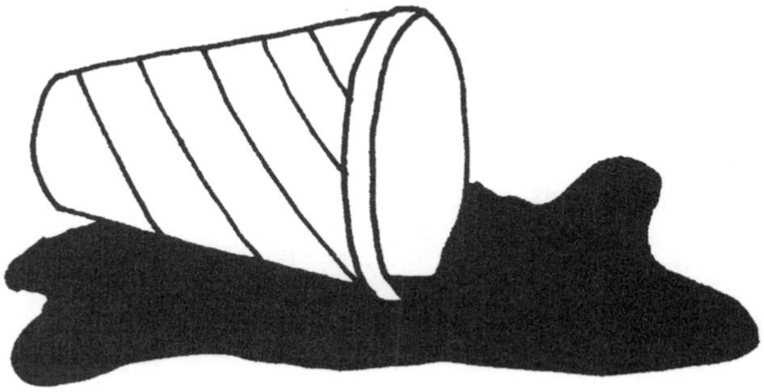

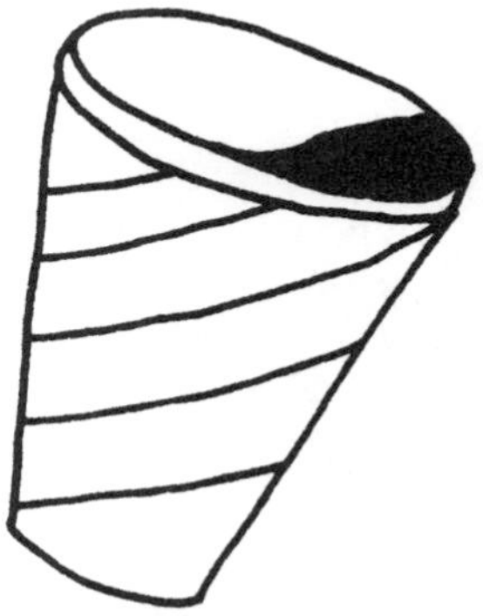

106 CD-3703

Name _____

✂ Cut out the pictures below and paste in order
from first to last.

1	2
3	4

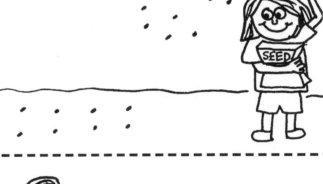

Name _____

✂ Cut out the pictures below and paste in order from first to last.

1	2
3	4

108

Name_____

✂ Cut out the pictures below and paste in order from first to last.

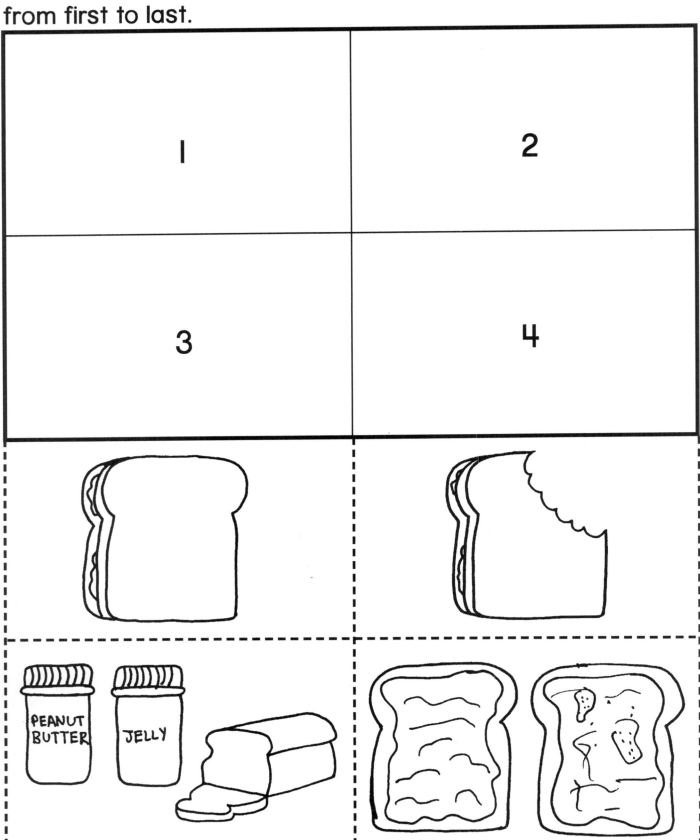

| 1 | 2 |
| 3 | 4 |

Name _____

✂ Cut out the pictures below and paste in order
from first to last.

1	2
3	4

110 CD-3703

Name_____

✂ Cut out the pictures below and paste in order from first to last.

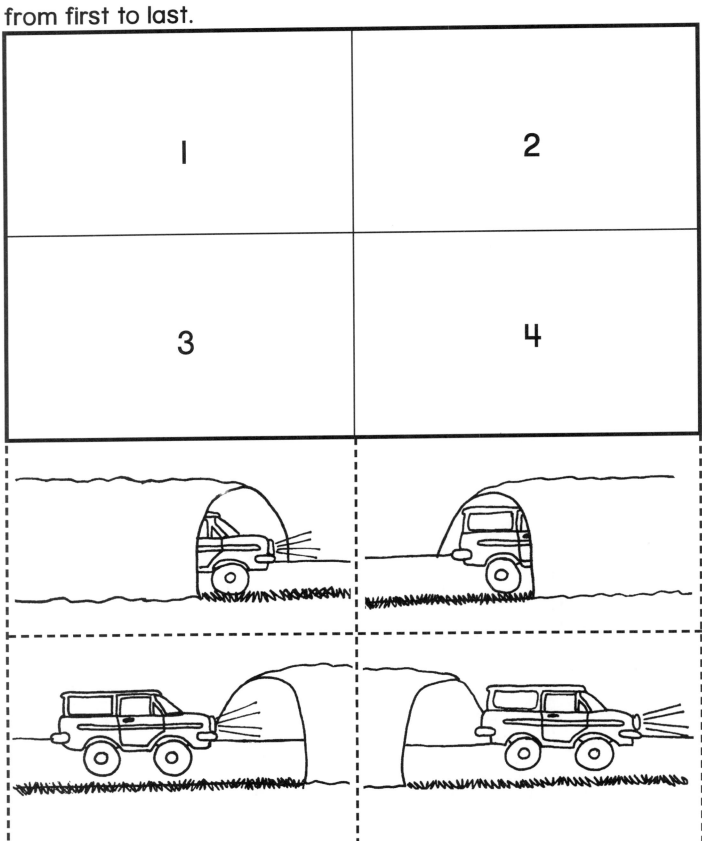

1	2
3	4

111   CD-3703

Name ____________________ Skill: Drawing and printing

Draw a picture of something fun to do in the spring time.

My favorite spring month is

Draw a picture of something you can do in the winter.

❄ ❄ ❄ ❄ ❄ ❄ ❄ ❄ ❄ ❄ ❄

❄ ❄ ❄ ❄ ❄ ❄ ❄ ❄ ❄ ❄ ❄

In the winter I like to

_____

- -

Name _____
Draw a picture of something you do in the **summer time.**

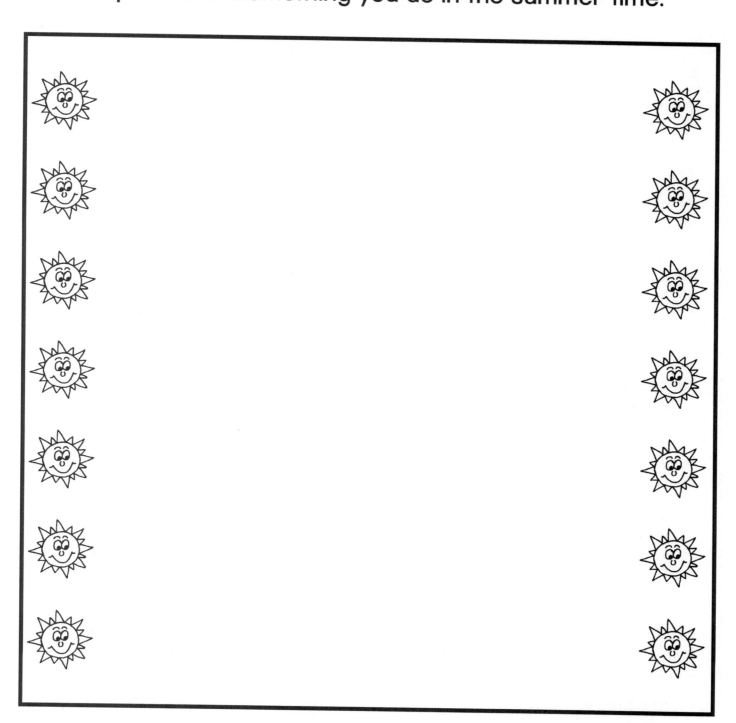

In the summer time it is fun to

_____

- -

114   CD-3703

Draw a picture of a fall activity.

My favorite fall activity is

_____

- -

_____

Name_____
Draw a picture of yourself in a rainy day outfit.

When it rains I like to wear my

_____

- -

_____

                   CD-3703

Name _____ Skill: Drawing and printing

Draw a picture of your favorite person.

My favorite person's name is

_____

- -

_____

117 CD-3703

Name _____

Draw a picture that shows your favorite movie.

My favorite movie is

_____

- -

_____

Draw a picture of your home.

My address is
_____

- -

_____

Skill: Drawing and printing

Draw a picture of someone talking on the telephone.

I know my telephone number. It is

_____

- -

_____

Name ________________________________ Skill: Drawing and printing

Draw a picture of your favorite animal.

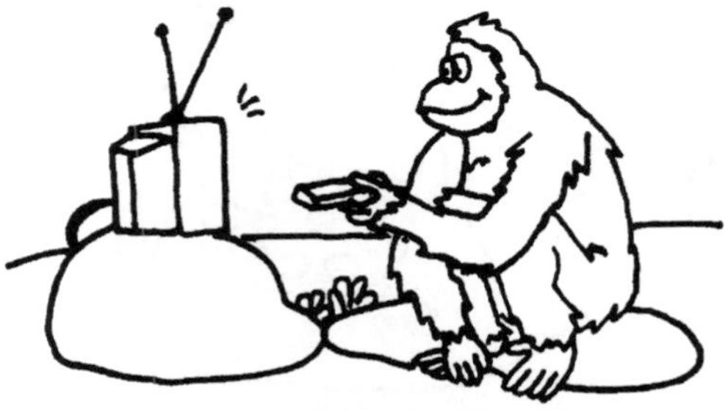

My favorite animal is a

____

- -

____

Name _____

Draw a picture of you and your family doing something fun together.

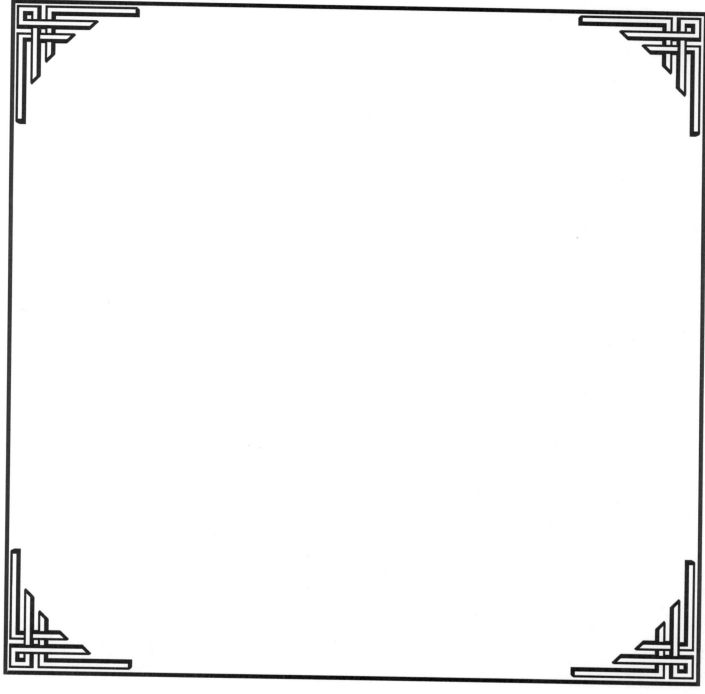

When my family is together we like to
_____

- -

Draw a picture of yourself.

SMILE!

My name is

_____

- -

123

Alphabet Award

A a
B b

_____

receives this award for

_____

Keep up the great work!

_____   _____
signed   date

I Know My Colors

_____

receives this award for

_____

Great Job!

Great Job!

_____   _____
signed   date

124   CD-3703

★ Numbers Award ★

_____

receives this award for

_____

Keep up the great work!

_____   _____
signed   date

I Know My Shapes

_____

receives this award for

_____

Great Job!

_____   _____
signed   date

Reproducible badges

Super Student!

Star Student!

We are proud of you!

_____

deserves this award for

_____

Keep up the great work!

_____   _____

signed   date

Alphabet, Colors, Numbers, and Shapes Certificate

This certifies that

_____

knows the alphabet, colors, numbers, and shapes and is entitled to receive this certificate

Given at _____

this _____ day of _____ 19____ .

A	B	C	D
E	F	G	H
I	J	K	L
M	N	O	P

0 1 2 3

4 5 6 7

8 9 10 11

12 13 14 15

Q	R	S	T
d	Z	W	X
Y	Z	a	b
c	d	e	f

16	17	18	19
20	21	22	23
24	25	26	27
28	29	30	31

g	h	i	j
k	l	m	n
o	p	q	r
s	t	u	v

32	33	34	35
36	37	38	39
40	50	60	70
80	90	100	+

W	X	Y	Z
one	two	three	four
five	six	seven	eight
nine	ten	eleven	twelve

thirty-seven thirty-three twenty-nine

thirty-eight thirty-four thirty

thirty-nine thirty-five thirty-one

forty thirty-six thirty-two

∨ ∧ = −

thirteen	fourteen	fifteen	sixteen
seventeen	eighteen	nineteen	twenty
twenty-one	twenty-two	twenty-three	twenty-four
twenty-five	twenty-six	twenty-seven	twenty-eight

forty-one	forty-two	forty-three	forty-four
forty-five	forty-six	forty-seven	forty-eight
forty-nine	fifty	sixty	seventy
eighty	ninety	one-hundred	

meditation
for life

meditation
for life

MARTINE BATCHELOR

photography *by* STEPHEN BATCHELOR

ECHO POINT BOOKS & MEDIA, LLC

to the memory of Liz Clayton
for a life well-lived

Published by Echo Point Books & Media
Brattleboro, Vermont
www.EchoPointBooks.com

Meditation for Life
ISBN: 978-1-64837-116-5 (casebound)
        978-1-62654-555-7 (paperback)

Set in Trebuchet and Wunderlich

Cover image: by Stephen Batchelor

Cover design by Rachel Gualco
Editorial and proofreading assistance by Ian Straus,
Echo Point Books & Media

contents

introduction

From a young age I was inspired by ideas of world peace, equality and love. But as I became an adult I realized that genuinely changing my feelings and thoughts, let alone changing the world, was going to take more than just good ideas. When I discovered Buddhism, it seemed to me that the practice of meditation could provide answers to my questions about how to live a better life.

In those days, in 1973, there was not much Buddhism around in the West. Here and there one could find groups based on various Eastern religions, which offered activities of a spiritual nature. I had begun by experimenting with energetic meditation, Sufi prayer, *ch'i-kung* exercises and even a Taoist correspondence course. Finally, I became interested in Buddhism, through a friend who was learning to meditate. Among his books were the *Platform Sutra* and the *Dhammapada*. The *Platform Sutra* introduced me to the radicalism of Zen ideas. However, it was the *Dhammapada*, with its pithy, direct and practical advice, that altered the course of my life. Instead of changing the world I decided to change myself, which seemed more realistic an endeavour. And I trusted that, in the end, the practice would also benefit others.

I was particularly attracted to the humour and playfulness of Chinese Zen Buddhism, but at that time it was difficult to visit China. While travelling in the East, I decided to fly to Japan to seek out Zen meditation there. By a happy turn of circumstance, a mistake on my plane ticket sent me to Tokyo via Seoul. I took the chance to visit Korea and discovered that there is also a strong tradition of Korean Zen. I was directed to Songgwangsa, the only temple to host foreigners, and after two weeks I decided to become a nun. Without the responsibility of a job or a partner, I felt it would be good to learn to meditate for a year or two. In the end I stayed for ten years! I benefited greatly from the Korean monastic format in which one meditates for ten hours a day for six months of the year, and studies or travels for the other six.

After nine years, Master Kusan, the resident teacher of Songgwangsa, died. I helped out with the transitional period and left Korea a year later. I decided to disrobe and become an ordinary person again; coming back to the West would be a way to put my Zen training into action. Conditions in a monastery are necessarily restricted in order to foster concentration, enquiry and a simple, dignified life. Becoming a layperson, marrying, living in a British Buddhist community and working as a house-cleaner provided me with great opportunities to apply in ordinary life what I had learnt during my ten years in Korea. Meeting these challenges enabled me to take meditation out of the meditation hall and make it a more organic part of my life.

This book is the result of the two experiences: ten years as a nun in Korea and fifteen years cleaning, teaching, listening, meditating and cultivating creative awareness in Devon. Its aim is to introduce the various aspects of meditation, from the sitting posture to meditative cooking, in an easy but comprehensive manner. I use the Buddhist framework because it is the one I am familiar with, and because I feel it can be easily presented without religious or exotic overtones. My aim is to offer various ideas, suggestions, techniques and reflections that will enable you to try out meditation for yourself. Doing so will help you to uncover and develop the qualities of compassion and wisdom that are already within you.

My hope is that this book is accessible without being over-simplified. I start with the basic techniques and ideas and try to move gently from there to notions of emptiness, interdependence and non-grasping. I have not followed any specific Buddhist school, but explain a variety of practices and ideas from different traditions, which I have found work for ordinary people in the modern world. Moreover, I have tried to look critically at each issue, be that ethics, the role of teachers or awakening. I want to encourage you to question and think for yourself. In Buddhist meditation faith is vital but the faith should be in yourself, in the world, in wisdom and compassion – not in a system or theory. This book is meant to be tested and applied as well as read. I have tried to put these ideas across in what I hope is a light and engaging manner.

Each chapter is divided into three parts. The first sets out the basic ideas behind Buddhist meditation. I try to explain both the theoretical underpinning of meditation and also how the principles of meditation work and can benefit you in your daily life. For example, in the first chapter I look at concentration and enquiry, which are at the heart of Buddhist meditation. I explain how concentration and enquiry are practised and show that they result in quietness and clarity. I also explain that by cultivating enquiry you will be able to free yourself from destructive and negative habits. We have a tendency to make up stories in our minds that are not necessarily true but may be either remnants from the past or created out of fear and insecurity. Meditation gently helps us to let these stories go. Finally, I have endeavoured to make the ideas I present in the first part of each chapter relevant to everyday experience.

The second part of each chapter is more technical and explains the nuts and bolts of meditation: how to do it, the different objects of concentration or enquiry, the attitude you should bring to meditation, and the obstacles you might encounter. This 'practice' section applies to formal meditation in the four postures (sitting, walking, standing and lying down), but I also try to explain how meditation can be applied informally, in ordinary life, and how it can help you with your feelings, thoughts, and the way you hold yourself and act in the world.

The third part of each chapter consists of a step-by-step guided meditation. It offers an easy-to-follow way of applying what has been discussed earlier in the chapter. When you use these sections you might want to have the book open next to you and read the instructions as you meditate. I would suggest you read one line at a time, trying to apply each instruction for a minute or two. Then read the next line and, again, apply the instruction for a couple of minutes. You could spend ten or twenty minutes each day doing these guided meditations,

whether in the morning, or in the evening, or in bed at night. One of the guided meditations is on conversation and another is on cooking. These are to be practised as you talk to a friend, or cook, and will give you some ideas about how you can meditate as you go about your day, working, relating and relaxing. I hope my book will inspire you to find many new ways of your own in which to involve meditation in your everyday life.

9

the heart of meditation

At the heart of Buddhist meditation is

concentration and enquiry. When you

cultivate these two qualities in meditation,

you develop your ability to be quiet and

clear and to offer understanding and love.

the heart of meditation

the buddha

Siddhartha Gautama, the Indian prince who was to become the Buddha – or 'Awakened One' – was born around 2,500 years ago in northeast India. While still a young man, Gautama developed a yearning to know the truth of existence. He renounced both his domestic life and his princely responsibilities, and left home to study for six years under the great spiritual teachers of his time. Although Gautama became accomplished in various methods of meditation, he was ultimately dissatisfied with them all. For no matter how deeply he meditated, he remained unable to resolve the mysteries and challenges of the human condition, with its problems of sickness, ageing and death.

So Gautama decided to leave his teachers and go his own way. For seven days he sat under a tree, meditating continuously. He finally reached awakening at dawn on the eighth day, at the moment he saw the morning star. In that instant, he became fully awakened. He realized the four noble truths: that there is suffering; the cause of suffering, which is craving; the cessation of suffering; and the path to accomplish the cessation of suffering. Gautama had completely dissolved the three poisons of hatred, greed and delusion, which are the causes of human anguish. From that moment on, he acted wisely and compassionately in his body, speech and mind. He saw that the root of suffering is craving, and that the way to extinguish craving is through the practice of meditation, ethics and wisdom. During the next fifty years, the Buddha – as he had now become – taught and helped others to see clearly and act compassionately. In doing so, he developed different types of meditation, each method suited to the needs of a particular person, group or circumstance.

Down the ages, great Buddhist teachers have developed many other methods of meditation, drawing on their own experience and understanding, and adapting the Buddhist religion and its practice of meditation to different times, places and cultures. Each strand of Buddhism developed in isolation, the practitioners largely unaware of any alternative approach. And, as is human nature, each school of Buddhist meditation became somewhat dogmatic and claimed that its method was the only true one.

The speed of travel and communication in the modern world, as well as the easy availability of books, means that we can now choose from a veritable profusion of Buddhist paths, each with their own meditational practices. Generally, each Buddhist group claims to possess the only true method of meditation, taught by the Buddha and transmitted down through the generations. And each, of course, lays claim to the most successful and direct route to awakening.

a choice of paths

Different schools of meditation developed from the Buddha's time onwards. All the Buddhist traditions focused on one aspect of his teachings and developed it further, so each school has its own emphasis and methods. In the West, you now find three main traditions. Tibetan Buddhism uses many different meditation methods, such as systematic reflection on death, visualization of mandalas, recitation of mantras and *dzogchen* ('great completion'), which puts the emphasis on awakening to the primordial buddha-mind within. The Zen tradition originated in China and spread to Korea and Japan. There are two main types of Zen meditation: one is based on *koans* (case stories provoking a Zen question), from the Rinzai school, the other is based on 'silent illumination', also known as 'just sitting', from the Soto school. Then there is the Theravada school of Southeast Asia, which developed in Thailand, Sri Lanka and Burma. The most popular meditation of this tradition is called *vipassana* ('insight'), which puts the emphasis on seeing clearly into the nature of things. Since it is not possible to practise all the different types of meditation at once, you have to make a choice. And this choice might depend on an accidental encounter with someone, on coming across an inspiring book, on a rational decision based on common sense, or simply, perhaps, on a gut feeling.

I myself was attracted to Zen Buddhism at an early age. It seemed practical, simple and to the point. In later years, I was introduced to the awareness practices of the Theravada tradition, and found them easy to relate to and effective. I also encountered Tibetan Buddhism, although I found its ceremonies too elaborate for my taste. Having said that, the multifaceted approach of Tibetan Buddhism, which places emphasis variously on devotion, colourful ritual and intellectual rigour, can suit a wide range of people.

However, one does not have to be a card-carrying Buddhist to practise Buddhist meditation. Not all Buddhists meditate and not all meditators are Buddhists! You can find Christian-Buddhists, Jewish-Buddhists and even agnostic Buddhists, who all practise meditation. The Buddha was very pragmatic and his teaching experiential. None of the meditations described in the following chapters requires you to believe in anything special or to belong to any specific religious group. The only requirement for meditation is the intention to be more awake, more aware, and to develop compassion and wisdom.

Because Buddhist meditation came from the East, it is important to distinguish between the Asian culture in which certain branches of Buddhism evolved and the method of meditation itself, inspired by the Buddha's teaching. To Westerners, some of the religious and cultural practices that accompany meditation seem strange. In fact, these practices often have little to do with either meditation or Buddhism. You could just let them go; or you might accept them in order to practise a meditation that you find useful. But if these cultural trappings hinder your progress, you should consider another method in which they are not so pronounced or distracting.

common sense

I once had an amusing brush with this business of cultural forms. Although I trained for ten years in the Korean Zen tradition, I have also visited Japanese and Taiwanese Zen temples. In Korean temples, even in the blazing heat of summer, it is considered polite to wear socks. In Japanese temples, however, the rule is not to wear socks unless they are ceremonial ones. Even if the temperature is well below freezing, you have to walk barefoot, with your feet sticking to the iced-up wooden boards. And in Taiwan it is different again; I noticed that the nuns sometimes wore socks and sometimes not. Naturally, I rejoiced in the thought that these women had reached the awakened state of 'socklessness' (not being attached to either wearing socks or not wearing them).

So, one day I ventured into a Taiwanese meditation hall completely sockless. At the end of the meditation period, however, I was taken aback when a nun scolded me for my bare feet. I pointed out that I had seen some nuns without socks, but she merely exclaimed: 'Only in the evening, when your feet are clean after washing. A Zen nun tries to wear socks at all times so that she can meditate deeply and pay true respects to the Buddha!' The moral is: in meditation, use your common sense. Adapt or let go according to the circumstances, and be wary of taking things too seriously or becoming excessively pious.

All types of Buddhist meditation consist essentially of two simple, timeless qualities: concentration and enquiry. Concentration helps you to develop stillness and calmness of mind. Enquiry helps you to cultivate a certain clarity and brightness of mind. Together, concentration and enquiry allow you to deepen your awareness until it becomes powerful and creative, enabling you to change in a playful manner and respond to life in a wiser, more compassionate way.

tibetan meditation

Concentration and enquiry, the two fundamental elements of Buddhist meditation, are deployed in different ways within each tradition. Tibetan Buddhists use a profusion of images and practices. One of their methods is to meditate on a certain theme, such as the nature of death.

meditation on death

In the meditation on death, there are three essential points of concentration. Firstly, there is the certainty of death. You reflect on all the people you know or have heard about who have died. Secondly, there is the uncertainty of the time of death. You consider the fact that people die at different ages and in different and unforeseen circumstances. Thirdly, you enquire into what, right now, are the most important things in your life, in light of the fact that death is certain but the time of its arrival uncertain. In this meditation, you concentrate, for thirty or forty minutes, exclusively on death.

The element of enquiry comes into play in the way that you try to look at both death and life in a different light. It is so easy for us to forget about death and this makes us depreciate the preciousness of life. By reflecting regularly on death, we become more conscious of it and what it truly means – that at some point we all have to die. At first, this

meditation might seem intellectual. But as you continue to practise, you will find it becomes more experiential, something you actually feel or experience and not just a mental act. Instead of fearing or ignoring death, you meet it head on. This not only changes the way you feel about death but also the way you view life, which becomes more vivid and precious.

visualization

Another method Tibetan Buddhists use is visualization. You visualize a complex three-dimensional image, or mandala. To hold this detailed image in your mind for any amount of time requires a high level of concentration. At the centre of the mandala, there is usually an image of a buddha or deity who embodies a certain awakened quality such as wisdom or compassion. While you are visualizing the image, you imagine yourself to be that buddha, sharing his degree of understanding and love. This is where enquiry comes in: for as long as you can identify with the central image, you will perceive and experience yourself in a radically different way. Indeed, you will open yourself to your full potential for understanding and love.

zen meditation

Zen is generally simpler than Tibetan Buddhism. It is often poetic although it still requires discipline. Zen has two main methods of meditation: questioning and silent illumination.

questioning

In the first Zen school, all you are required to do is ask a question. In Korea, one of the most common questions asked by meditators is 'What is this?'. As you sit in meditation, you simply repeat: 'What is this? What is this?'. The element of concentration comes in the way you return to the question whenever you are distracted from it. The element of enquiry makes you ask each question deeply. Rather than endlessly repeating the question like a mantra, you ask because you genuinely do not know the answer. This practice helps you to open up to the unknowable, to the great mystery of life.

It enables your mind to become more quiet and flexible. You start to wonder and marvel at life instead of always trying to fix it or make it more solid.

silent illumination

The other Zen school employs the method of silent illumination. Meditating with silent illumination simply involves sitting still without doing anything at all. Your concentration is focused on the moment itself, so that you are wide open to its multitude of emotions, thoughts, sensations, sounds, tastes and smells. Enquiry enables you to be in the moment without being attached to it, without grasping, fabricating stories, day-dreaming, regretting or planning. You just are — and in that instant your mind can shine through brightly.

theravadan meditation

One of the most popular forms of Theravadan meditation among Westeners is *vipassana* ('insight'), in which the main emphasis is on awareness. You concentrate on being as aware as possible of a certain object or sensation, such as the breath, a sound, a thought, a sensation in the body. Enquiry is focused on the characteristics of existence that the Buddha pointed out: change, unreliability and non-self. For example, people tend to think that whatever *is* will continue to *be* for a certain amount of time. But in Theravada meditation you notice that, in fact, things change from moment to moment. Sounds, sensations and thoughts are never exactly the same for long but are in a constant state of flux. With practice you come to appreciate this fact and live your life from a perspective of accepting and flowing with change.

concentration

Concentration is essential in Buddhist meditation and helps to calm the mind, although it must be emphasized that its function is not to stop the thought process. The aim of meditation is not to make your mind blank or empty, but to make it more supple and peaceful. Concentrating on something such as the breath does not narrow or tense the attention. On the contrary, you steadily but gently rest your attention on your breathing, as you attune yourself to the breath and try to become one with it.

As you attempt to concentrate, you will find that your mind is easily distracted. It is important to remember your intention to be aware and awake, and to keep returning to the object of concentration. This focus will act as an anchor to the immediate experience, to reality. Keep returning to your breathing and your mind will become calmer as you give less power to your worries, fears, hopes and dreams. These are created by thoughts, which have a tendency to be repetitive, spinning faster and faster as they proliferate into a web of heavier, darker, more excited thoughts. By returning to a consideration of what sensations or sounds are in themselves, you can stem the flow of energy to the causes of agitation and let your mind rest in a more still and peaceful state.

You have to be careful not to criticize or fight the mind, since it is normal to think, hear sounds and feel sensations. Simply focus on the object of concentration while maintaining an open awareness. As you pay steady attention to your breathing, you will also be aware of sounds and thoughts. The trick is not to grasp or reject them. Just leave them alone and let them come and go lightly.

17

If you do become distracted, notice it and come back gently to your breathing. The aim of meditation is to create longer intervals of awareness. What is important is not how long you focus on your breathing but how soon you return to it from a distraction. When you start to meditate, you might find you focus for only a few seconds and then are distracted for ten minutes. After some practice, the gap narrows: a few minutes focused on breathing followed by a few minutes spent day-dreaming. Finally, you will find that stray thoughts or images distract you from concentrating on your breathing for only a few seconds.

The better you can concentrate, the fewer causes of agitation there will be and the more peaceful your mind will become. If you choose to think, you can do so – rigorously and clearly focused. If you want to let go of a thought you can do that too. Your mind becomes free and you will treat it as a friend, rather than a burden or an enemy.

By practising concentration, the mind and body become more relaxed and at ease. But you need to be careful not to become lethargic or 'spaced out'. You are not trying to escape into some sort of rarefied state of abstraction. On the contrary, to meditate you need to be alert and present in yourself. This is where the element of enquiry becomes important. Enquiry counterbalances concentration. It gives energy, sharpness and vividness to meditation.

enquiry

Enquiry is not necessarily intellectual. It harnesses the mind's natural ability to be bright, illuminating and perceptive.

Enquiry involves looking deeply into your own experience, perceptions and thoughts, and recognizing and questioning them. People are generally set in their ways when it comes to perceiving the world and themselves. They tend to act and react in the same pattern, which causes pain both to themselves and to others. Enquiry gives true insight into what is happening. It will make you examine how you are feeling, thinking and behaving, and lead you to question the causes and effects of your actions.

Enquiry helps you to see that you are not as fixed and constrained as you often feel you are. It can free you from your destructive or negative habits and allow your positive qualities to shine through. Enquiry does not judge or moralize and force you to stop doing something. On the contrary, enquiry frees you creatively, presenting choices in a light, sparkling way. You will be tempted to laugh when you recognize your personal foibles, which will then become like difficult friends, who you accept and love while being aware of their ways and how to handle them. Or you will put your foibles in perspective instead of letting them grow into frightening and incapacitating monsters.

Whereas concentration settles you down and diminishes tension, enquiry brings a dash of zest to life. You will find yourself willing to experiment and play with your thoughts, experiences and circumstances. You will open yourself up to life and its potential. Together, these two qualities are liberating. They help you to lighten your inner landscape and make you creatively responsive to your outer environment.

p r a c

basic meditation

the half-lotus position

the Burmese position

Buddhist meditation is usually practised in one of four positions: sitting, walking (see pages 35 to 36), lying down (see pages 63 to 64) and standing (see page 137).

Sitting normally takes place on the floor in various cross-legged positions, such as the lotus (see pages 22 and 122), the half-lotus, the quarter-lotus and the Burmese. You generally use two cushions: one square and thin, the other round and fat. The square cushion helps you sit more comfortably on the floor. The round cushion can be used to raise your bottom so that your knees rest on the square one.

the sitting position

In the lotus position, ankles and feet – soles facing upwards – are placed on the thighs. This is hard to do and not recommended unless you are adept at yoga. In the half-lotus position, one foot only is raised up on the thigh, while the other is tucked beneath the thigh. In the quarter-lotus, the raised foot rests closer to the knee. And, finally, in the Burmese position, the lower parts of the legs are both placed on the floor, with one foot underneath the opposite thigh and one foot against the opposite knee. You could also kneel on the floor with a cushion between your legs; or kneel with your legs tucked beneath a wooden bench.

All these postures can be painful for Westerners who are not used to sitting on the floor. A good alternative is to sit on a chair (see page 92), keeping your back straight, if possible without leaning against the chair. You could adjust your posture by placing cushions under your bottom and feet. It is important in sitting meditation that your posture is erect, but not rigidly so. You should open out your shoulders and feel your neck resting lightly between them. Try imagining the back of your head gently elongating towards the sky.

eyes shut or open?

Your hands should rest lightly on each other or on your knees. Try to sit with your whole body relaxed. The eyes, however, present a problem because the three Buddhist traditions differ over what to do with them. In Theravadan *vipassana* meditation, they are closed; in Zen, half-closed, and in the Tibetan *dzogchen* tradition, wide open. My advice is to keep your eyes closed if you feel restless, open if you feel sleepy, and half-closed otherwise. It is essential not to tense them in any way. Whether half-closed or wide open, do not focus on anything but let your eyes gaze gently. In short, do not worry about them – just let them be.

There are many different instructions regarding sitting meditation. But, in the final analysis, every person is unique, with his or her particular set of physical characteristics. You have to find the right posture for you – the one which allows you to sit as comfortably as possible. Most people are not used to sitting completely still even for a short period of time. The body and the mind need to get used to it.

kneeling with a bench

21

Although you are bound to feel a certain amount of physical discomfort after sitting for a while (especially if you are a beginner), you will probably be able to learn to cope. However, if you continue to experience pain for some time after a period of sitting meditation has finished, you need to find a more comfortable position.

the full lotus position

breathing

Once you have established a comfortable sitting posture, you can begin meditating by concentrating on your breathing. First be aware of it; ask yourself how you know you are breathing. Feel the sensation of cool air passing through your nostrils and going down into your lungs; feel your abdomen expanding and warmer air coming out of your nostrils. The best place to feel the air is at the nostrils and where the abdomen rises and falls. At the start of your meditation, try concentrating on either of these two places.

For your first meditation, you may decide to meditate for ten minutes or so. During that time your intention should be to pay as much attention as you can to your breathing. What usually happens is something like this: you focus on the first breath, the second one and the third – and then you hear a sound and wonder about it. If this happens, remember your intention to be aware of your breathing. Then you will reconnect with your breathing for a few seconds . . . until you start to worry about tomorrow's dinner or your shopping.

Catch yourself and remember that your intention is to be aware now, to be in this moment and not to think about the past or future, even if only for ten minutes. Allow yourself to be aware, to be totally present in this precious and unrepeatable moment, by focusing on your breathing. After ten minutes, stretch your legs and gently stand up, preserving your peaceful frame of mind for as long as possible.

guided meditation: breathing

- Sit comfortably with your back straight but relaxed.

- Take a few deep breaths, then let the breath flow out naturally.

- Rest your attention on the rhythm of your breathing and on the air you breathe.

- Do not imagine your breathing, do not visualize it. Just experience it.

- Do not control your breathing, making it more deep or shallow. Just be aware of your breathing as it is, from moment to moment.

- If you become distracted, remember your intention to be aware, to rest in the present. Come back to your breathing gently and firmly again and again.

- Do not be annoyed by your distracted thoughts. Just notice them and return to concentrating on your breathing as soon as you can.

- Focus on your breathing but maintain an open awareness. You may hear sounds, feel sensations, think thoughts. Do not grasp at them, make stories out of them or reject them. Just let them come and go lightly.

- As your mind becomes quiet and still, look more deeply into your breathing and the air that you breathe through your nostrils and all the pores of your body.

- Consider that every human being is breathing the same air. It goes into other people's lungs and comes out again, then goes into your lungs and out again, and so the process continues. Experience that connection.

- Trees and plants are involved in creating the air you breathe. Animals are breathing the same air. Focus on your breathing and look deeply into it; experience that connection fully.

- Come back to your breathing, come back to the world.

- Be one with your breathing, be one with the world.

- Rest in awareness, be intimately connected to the whole world.

- Open your eyes, relax your back and your legs, and stand up gently.

creative awareness

One of our greatest gifts is awareness, yet we
often live as if we were half-asleep. Creative
awareness is about waking up to life, to all
its choices and possibilities for change. The
root of creative awareness is acceptance.

creative awareness

wake up to life!

Meditation is not an end in itself. Meditation is a tool, a method to help you achieve an end. You are neither trying to reach a rarefied meditative state nor speculating intellectually on the nature of existence. As you meditate, try to cultivate concentration and enquiry. These two qualities will help you to develop quietness and clarity, which in turn will enable you to become more creatively aware.

One of your greatest gifts as a human being is to be aware – to perceive, recognize and respond to your environment. But it seems that most of the time we prefer to function on automatic pilot, living our lives half-aware, even half-asleep. Meditation is about waking up to every moment.

In meditation, concentration brings you back to awareness and enables you to be more spacious in your actions and reactions. Like a room full of furniture, our mental and emotional processes are often cluttered and busy. The aim of concentration is to help the mind feel as free as empty space. Enquiry makes you curious and playful. It prompts you to question what is going on, to ask yourself about the causes of whatever you are feeling, thinking and doing, and what the

effects of these feelings, thoughts and actions are likely to be. Meditation is a journey of self-discovery. However, having awareness means more than blankly observing. On the contrary, awareness is about creatively engaging with your experience as it arises. When you have a thought, a feeling or a sensation, when you encounter an object, a person or a situation, you meet and know them fully. Instead of passively submitting, lost in your contact with the experience and blind to what is really going on, you engage actively and respond creatively. That is why I call it 'creative' awareness.

self-interest

I had been meditating for a few months in Korea when, one day, I suddenly realized that everything I did was out of self-interest. I used to be a new age anarchist so would have given the shirt off my back to anybody who asked for it. Until then, I had been convinced that I was one of the most compassionate people in the world. But as I sat in meditation I became more aware of what I was really doing and why. In the meditation hall, I could not distract myself. I could not escape by reading or watching television. I just sat there, hour after hour, day after day, and everything became much clearer. I realized that I was as self-interested as anyone else. I also realized that the problem was not just with me and that everybody else was also acting in the same self-interested way. At the time, I was living in a small room with four other nuns. I noticed that if our self-interests coincided, we were fairly pleasant and peaceful. However, if they did not, we became resentful of each other and argumentative.

Creative awareness does not mean judging and condemning. It means seeing things clearly and at the same time spaciously and lightly. It means realizing that we are like butterflies

fluttering about, trying to get the best nectar and sweetest flowers. This new awareness did not make me feel bad; I found it funny. I saw that life is like a dance, a play. Awareness helped me to become humbler and less full of myself. I understood that I was just like everybody else: no better, no worse. When I was young I wanted, as everybody in some way wants, to be special, to be different. Meditation makes you realize that you are ordinary — and that the beauty of ordinariness is that it connects you to everybody else.

accept yourself

At the root of creative awareness is acceptance. You become conscious of what constitutes you: your good qualities, bad qualities, skills and limitations. You become able to recognize and appreciate your positive aspects: your kindness, humour and intelligence, your joyful or reflective nature, your abilities to hear, see, feel and communicate. You become more confident, able to affirm that you are good at certain things, that there are situations in which you perform well. Through this knowing and appreciation you can cultivate your good qualities even more. You realize that actually you neither need nor want to become someone else. You can work on what you were born with and what you have become. It can be a pleasure to know yourself.

Creative awareness also enables you to see your weaknesses and limitations clearly. If you stop being blind to your weaknesses and accept them, they will no longer be able to trip you up. You will become aware of certain negative patterns, maybe a tendency to be impatient, angry or jealous, to jump to conclusions, or become easily depressed and negative about yourself. In general, one is either blind to these tendencies or totally overpowered by them. With meditative awareness, it is possible to understand negative patterns and so have the motivation to work with them creatively.

let go of stories

It is easy to get lost in emotions and thoughts. We are inclined to make up stories about ourselves, other people and situations, which are not always accurate. These stories are built up over time from an accumulation of our fears, memories, expectations and ideals, and also from what is said and expected of us by family and society. Caught up in the story line you are spinning in your head, you become unaware of your body and your surroundings. You get absorbed in telling yourself that you are right and someone else is wrong, in asking yourself: 'How could he do this to me?' The story can go on and on as you connect what is happening now to other, past events. Stop and think about what you are doing to yourself. What is happening to your body? Perhaps you are moving agitatedly, pacing up and down the room. Is your heart beating faster, are your limbs trembling?

I used to get angry and self-righteous quite often until one day I noticed what I was doing to myself. I was having a discussion with a fellow community member that had turned into a polite but tense argument. She said that I never made beds for guests. I replied that I had been unable to do them recently but intended to fulfil my duties from then on. She did not believe me. At the same time, I had to start cooking lunch for fifteen people. So I cut short the discussion and began work. I was dicing carrots rather dangerously, going over in my mind what had been said and getting more and more angry until I suddenly became aware that my heart was beating fast and my legs were shaking. It occurred to me then that it was I, and nobody else, who was creating these painful effects. When I stopped to look into my thoughts, a refrain clearly appeared: 'I am right and she is wrong!' I realized that this fellow community member must also be saying to herself: 'I am right and she is wrong!' At that moment I saw that we were both right and wrong, and this instantly enabled me to let go of the negative feelings and thoughts, and finish cooking the meal safely.

break negative habits

Creative awareness gives you the choice to act differently and provides a space for transformation to occur. You can break out of your negative patterns of behaviour by asking yourself whether you want to continue creating and perpetuating the same suffering, or whether you want to experiment with a different way of behaving.

By remembering meditation techniques such as returning again and again to focus on your breathing, you can activate the concentration that prevents you from getting lost in thoughts and emotions. With concentration you can diminish the obsessive hold of an imaginary story line. You can also break out of negative patterns by cultivating enquiry, which shines light on the situation at hand. By making you look deeply at what is going on right now, enquiry allows you to see things differently and more wisely. However, it takes time for meditation to work at that deep a level. You need to build the power of creative awareness by meditating regularly. Over time, stillness and clarity will be developed and you will be surprised at the habits and patterns you recognize and are able to shed like old, worn-out clothes.

One of my patterns, developed early in childhood, was to cut people off if they did something I did not like. This would go on for days and sometimes weeks. When I began to meditate, I found that the time I spent cutting people off was reduced, until one day I actually caught myself before I did it. I immediately realized that here was an opportunity to try to do something different. The feeling that followed was fear of the unknown. Behaving in a way in which I had never behaved before was nearly unthinkable! Eventually my creative awareness gave me the impetus to try. Instead of giving the friend who had hurt me the cold shoulder, I turned to her and smiled. At once I felt utter ease and then a few stings of conscience that I had not tried something so easy before. I realized that I had been so accustomed to a certain pattern of behaviour that, unconsciously, I preferred the familiarity of the suffering I knew to the uncertainty of an unknown peace. I also thought about what it might have been like to be on the receiving end of this habit, and recognized how much suffering I must have been causing other people. Totally caught up in my own behaviour, I had been unable to see outside of the pattern and could only perpetuate it.

use creative awareness

Creative awareness can be applied in many different contexts. When you go for a walk in the countryside, you usually start off intending to enjoy nature: the fresh air, the beautiful

coastline, the delicate flowers, the trees swaying in the wind. However, it is easy to slip quickly into thinking about something else: a problem at the office, your shopping list, what you are going to eat for dinner, or some other concern. You do not see the blue of the sea and the pinkness of the flowers. Your body is walking but your mind is somewhere else. Creative awareness jolts you into remembering to be present. Looking directly and deeply at what is in front of your eyes and feet, you notice the shimmering quality of the sea, the vividness of a wild flower. Everything appears with an extraordinary brightness and clarity. The things around you have not become special but because you have taken off your usual blindfold you relate to them in a special way. The more you cultivate meditation the more this special way will become natural.

at work

You can bring creative awareness to physical work by observing how you use your body. This will help you develop more effective ways of moving, standing and sitting. I love gardening but it took me some time to realize that I could not force my body to garden willy-nilly. I would get sciatica every time I gardened, until I really began to observe my movements and found a softer way of digging and weeding.

Creative awareness will show you different ways of working. Sitting at your desk in front of your computer screen, this awareness will remind you to be careful of your posture and, if your head feels fuzzy, to stand up or go out for a few minutes. When you are working with a team, it will help you to relate to each member of that team creatively and kindly. You might be so intent on achieving a goal that you are constantly ahead of yourself, already at the end of one task and thinking of the next. With the help of meditation, try to stay steadily and efficiently with the task at hand and you will enjoy the work so much more. Working in a mechanical fashion, with the body there and the mind elsewhere, in the past or the future, is not very fulfilling – and automatic, unaware actions can lead to accidents.

Perhaps you feel resentful because your job is not valued, or you personally consider it a 'low' kind of work. When I returned from Korea and became a layperson, I had to find paid work and all I could do was house-cleaning. It was a real comedown as I used to be this 'important nun' – and furthermore had never been a great lover of housework. However, I had no choice. Luckily, I found that through practising meditation I could accept very quickly what I was doing as just 'work'. My job was useful; if I was present and accepting of it I could do it well, and then there was the satisfaction of a job well done. As human beings, we need to be active, to be doing. If you work with creative awareness instead of day-dreaming, are present to your thoughts and actions and inhabit fully each moment of work, there is a flow and a rightness in whatever you do. Every action is as it should be. There are no highs or lows – there is just creating and doing.

in relationships

Relationships can be nurturing but they can also be very difficult. Creative awareness lets you see the problems in your relationships clearly. We often relate to people only on certain conditions; we ask them to fulfil our needs or to be exactly as we want them to be. But the beauty of a relationship – be it with a partner, a friend, a child, a relative – is that it enables you to open to another person, and that person to you. With creative awareness, you become more aware and appreciative of other people. You see them as they are, not as you imagine them or want them to be. You recognize their good qualities but you also see their foibles and have space for those too: you begin to love them unconditionally. Acceptance is the ground of love. When you are totally accepted by another person you get an incredibly enriching feeling of trust and appreciation, and you do not need to be afraid of becoming more intimate. From this basis of acceptance, you can discuss any difficulties or differences. You are no longer opponents fighting over territory but true friends trying to understand and help each other as you grow together.

within yourself

Creative awareness is also useful because it shows how the mind influences the body and, conversely, how the body influences the mind. When you are feeling cranky and irritable, try to work out the real reason. Is the whole world really against you? Are you really annoyed because the weather is terrible or the kitchen is in a mess? You might feel that you cannot stand it for a moment longer, and that it is all the fault of so and so! But turn inwards and look at what you are actually feeling. Are you tired after a busy week? Have you been pushing yourself too far because you have too much to do? Stop! Your body is tired and you need to relax, perhaps to lie down for thirty minutes. What makes most sense? To continue to be irritated and maybe explode at someone whose only fault is being there, or to rest for half an hour, do a little less for this one day, and then be more kind and spacious to yourself and others for the rest of the week?

Concentration, enquiry and creative awareness will help you create the space in your mind to notice what is actually happening to you and, if necessary, enable you to change the situation. With creative awareness, you will become actively engaged with life. You will not passively endure and react according to misguided impulses – instead you will be able to work, practise, experiment and enjoy your life, seeing it as play rather than as a burden.

Once, I spent a whole day in the home of Godwin Samaratne, a meditation teacher who lived in Kandy, Sri Lanka. His house was very small and the living room gave directly onto the street as well as onto the adjoining bedroom, kitchen and bathroom. It was lovely to watch him going unhurriedly through his day, writing letters, taking a shower, all the while being interrupted constantly by various people – beggars, friends and Western visitors. He responded to everyone with kindness and attention, and still managed to do what he had to do. As I was waiting, seated on a sofa, I meditated and relaxed as I watched his creative awareness in action. His life was totally public, yet at the same time he had found a gentle way of taking care of himself.

p r a c

more basic meditation

There are different ways to meditate by concentrating on sensations in the body.

contact sensations

One is to pay attention to your ability to feel, sense and have contact. Focus on the sensation of your hands touching each other, of your buttocks in contact with the cushion or chair, of your clothes against your skin, or of the coolness or warmth of air on your face.

strong sensations

Another method is to pay attention to strong sensations in the body. You might be bothered by an itch on your cheek, or if you are sitting cross-legged you might feel pain in your knee or ankle. Just observe the feeling of itching or pain as it is; do not grasp or reject it. If you sit utterly still and do not scratch as you usually would but instead look deeply into the itch, it will not have the unbearable feel of 'I have to scratch this or else!' and it will disappear quickly by itself.

sweeping the body

The third method is what is called 'sweeping the body' meditation. Start at the top of the head and observe any sensations there – in the scalp, the face, the jaw. Notice how it feels to have a head. Then move to the neck, the shoulders, the torso (back and front), the arms and hands, the pelvic area, the thighs and knees, the lower parts of the legs and the feet. For a few

minutes be aware of your whole body, and then slowly go back up through the different parts of the body again. At first, it might be easier to go slowly and spend five minutes on each part of the body. This method is good for people who have trouble concentrating, as the regular change of focus makes the meditation feel more lively.

When you meditate on sensations, you do not create or imagine them, you do not worry or speculate about them. You just observe your sensations, impartially but intently. You become interested in experiencing the process of sensation. We are so often lost in thoughts and distractions that we forget about our bodies. Through this meditation you become aware of your body from moment to moment and grateful for the amazing gift of the ability to sense and feel.

enquiry through sensations

There are also different ways of enquiring while you meditate on sensations. Enquiring does not mean thinking as such. It can be better compared to focusing a beam of the mind's light on a specific point of your experience.

go into the pain

Take, for example, a pain in the knee that starts to bother you while you are sitting in meditation. When you feel this sort of pain, the first thing you do is identify with it, describing it to yourself as 'my pain' in 'my knee'. You characterize the feeling as painful and unpleasant, and immediately want to be rid of it. However, once the mind has been quietened through concentration, you can use enquiry to go into the feeling in your knee, experiencing the sensation for itself. Then you will feel the pain differently, as a simple vibrating sensation that moves about and changes in intensity from moment to moment. You can deal with an itch in the same way. Go into the itch with your focused beam of mental enquiry and experience it as nothing more than a faintly pulsating sensation.

notice changes

If you do not enquire into your sensations, you might perceive them as unbearably intense, and presume they will continue to be so for a long time. However, if you do enquire into your sensations, you will soon notice their evanescent nature. Sensations differ in intensity from second to second, they might disappear totally within minutes. The realization that sensations come and go will allow you to break your tendency to 'permanentize' and assume that things are more lasting and painful than they could ever really be.

feel the contact

If the body is at ease and there are no strong feelings, then enquire into the bare sensation of contact. Notice the feeling of contact of your hands with each other, or of your buttock with the cushion. Where does one hand finish and the other begin? Where does the buttock stop and the cushion start? Notice the seamlessness of the experience: there is just contact. This enquiry helps you to dissolve your rigid tendency to fix and solidify things. It allows you to realize that experience is fluid, in constant motion.

the walking position

If you have difficulty sitting for long periods of time, walking is an alternative meditation posture that is quite easy. There are three different methods of walking meditation, which are all practised on a predetermined course: walking slowly back and forth for a short distance; walking at a normal pace on a longer, circular route; and walking fast for a longer distance or in a wide circle.

If you are a beginner at walking meditation, it is easiest to concentrate while walking slowly. Choose a patch of ground, about ten metres long, on which you can walk back and forth for ten or twenty minutes.

When you begin the walking meditation, first stand still for a minute or two, aware of the body in this standing position. Be careful to keep your back straight but not rigid and your eyes gently opened, looking ahead and

the walking position

not fixing on the feet or anything else. Then start to walk, lifting one foot, then putting it down; lifting the other foot, then putting it down; walking slowly over the ten metres. Stop and turn, and again stand for a few seconds, aware of your whole body. Then start again, one foot after the other, noticing all the time bodily movements such as the lifting of the leg, the positioning of the foot, the sensation of the ground underfoot.

It is essential to alternate sitting meditation with walking meditation. Walking meditation helps restore a more fluid and lively energy to the body. It also refreshes the mind, especially if you walk outside. You are not going anywhere, you are walking just for the sake of walking.

Walking meditation is an art! It helps to break the patterns you might fall into whenever you walk. Do you have a tendency to be distracted, to think of something else as you walk from a to b? Do you project yourself ahead and arrive before you have even started the journey? Or can you walk meditatively and mindfully, aware of your body and mind in the moment, open to the present?

guided meditation: sensations

- Sit as solidly as a mountain and as spaciously as an ocean.

- First pay attention to sensations in and around the head: on your scalp, your face, inside your skull.

- How does it feel to have a head? Do not imagine or visualize sensations, just observe what is there.

- Move your focus gently to the neck and the shoulders. Watch any sensations without grasping at them or rejecting them.

- Now, move the attention to the torso, front and back. Notice the feel of your clothes against your skin.

- Next, take the awareness to the arms and the hands. Feel the contact of your hands with each other or with your knees.

- Expand the focus to the pelvic area, front and back. Experience the contact of your buttocks with the cushion.

- At the level of sensations, where does buttock stop and cushion start? Feel the seamlessness of this experience.

- Move the awareness to the thighs and the knees. If there is any painful sensation, look deeply into the bare experience of it.

- Now focus your attention on the lower part of the legs, the ankles and the feet. Notice how sensations do not remain exactly the same from moment to moment.

- Finally, be aware of the whole body.

- What is the immediate experience of having a body? Feel the actual physicality of it, not what you might imagine it is like.

- Come back to sensations, come back to awareness. Recognize and appreciate your ability to feel, to sense.

- As you end the meditation, rest in quietness and clarity. After you get up, pay gentle attention to sensations as you move and go about your day.

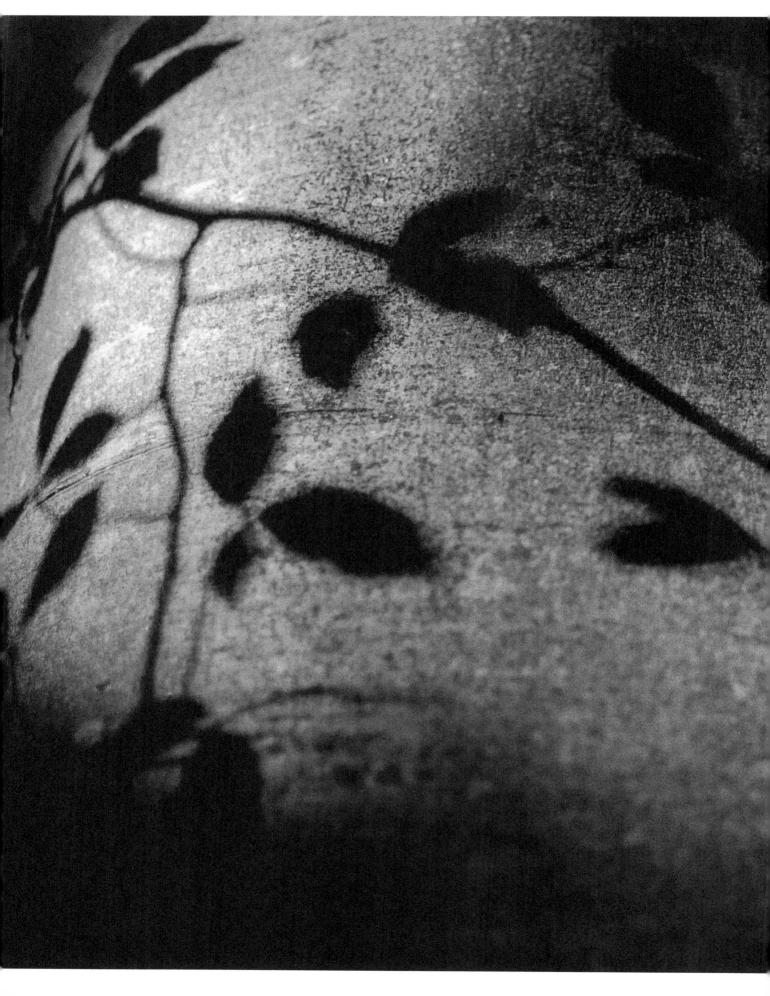

inspiration

The inspiration to meditate is not external to you but internal; it is not why you begin to meditate but why you continue to meditate — it is not what draws you along the path, but the path itself.

inspiration

why meditate?

'Why do you meditate?' 'What inspires you?' 'Why should I meditate?' I have been asked these questions many times. Early on, I realized that the best answer to all of them is: 'To meditate is enough in itself.' As it is not an intellectual exercise, the meaning of meditation is revealed simply by practising it. Indeed, what we think about meditation is often quite different from the experience. And so, the inspiration for meditation is meditation itself.

inspiration to begin

Everyone who meditates will have a different story about what inspired them to begin. My own teacher, Master Kusan, was born into a Buddhist family but had no particular interest in meditation until he became very ill. Then, at the suggestion of a Buddhist friend, he went to a hermitage, hoping to be cured by reciting the mantra associated with compassion and healing, *om mani padme hum*. He had to recite the mantra every day for a hundred days and, though he had not initially been entirely convinced by his friend's advice, by the end of the period he was cured. This experience inspired him to begin practising meditation and become a monk.

When he began his first retreat, Master Kusan made a vow that for the sake of all beings he would become awakened by the end of three months. During this retreat he meditated day and night, but no matter how hard he tried he could not achieve awakening. Still plagued by thoughts and dreams, still agitated and confused, he became despondent and asked himself whether life would be worth living if he were not awakened. At that moment, he had a vision of the Himalayas, and realized that it was presumptuous of him to think he could attain awakening in three months when it had taken the Buddha six years. He told me that, thereafter, his faith and inspiration were unshakeable.

The story of Master Kusan's teacher is even more remarkable. Master Hyobong was a Korean High Court judge who during the Japanese occupation was faced with having to pass the death sentence on a Korean freedom fighter. Unable to accept what he had to do, he vanished overnight, leaving everything behind to wander the countryside in search of an honest way of life. Visiting a Buddhist temple, he was inspired to become a monk. He was already thirty-nine years old when he began to meditate. For him, it was a matter of great urgency

40

to awaken and he became famous for his hard practice, even getting the nickname 'leathery buttocks'.

changing motivation

When I reflect on what inspires me to meditate, I see that my motivation has changed over time. It all started when I read a passage in the *Dhammapada*. The passage pointed out that before you could change others you had to change yourself:

If he makes himself as good as he tells others to be, then in truth he can teach others. Difficult indeed is self-control.

Until then, I had been very active politically, full of ideas about changing the world into a more peaceful and egalitarian place. When I read that passage, it occurred to me that I could not hope to change the world if I could not even change my own negative thoughts and painful feelings. Yet in the *Dhammapada*, the Buddha implies that through meditation it is possible to transform one's state of mind and oneself.

Reading this passage spurred me on to look for a teacher and a method, so I travelled East. As soon as I arrived at his monastery in Korea, Master Kusan suggested that I become a nun. I hesitated for a few days, finally convincing myself that maybe this would be a good opportunity, for a year or two, to learn exotic Eastern arts like *t'ai chi* and calligraphy, and to try out some meditation too. In the end, I stayed for ten years, did not do any *t'ai chi* or calligraphy, and the only thing I learnt about was meditation. After a while, I began to meditate for its own sake, without aiming at any particular goal.

Meditation is its own inspiration because it is food for the spirit. You have to eat every day to sustain your body and, in the same way, you need meditation to nurture your spirit. What impels you to meditation is your inner being, who needs quietness and clarity, being instead of doing. Meditation gives you the opportunity to live a full human life; one where you express and act on all your goodness and wisdom. When you meditate you feel at home, you return to your original being.

faith to be free

I believe that an act of meditation is actually an act of faith – of faith in your spirit, in your own potential. Faith is the basis of meditation. Not faith in something outside you – a metaphysical buddha, or an unattainable ideal, or someone else's words. The faith is in yourself, in your own 'buddha-nature'. You too can be a buddha, an awakened being that lives and responds in a wise, creative and compassionate way.

When you begin to meditate, you might feel separate from your faith, which is more like a belief. You might think it is a good idea to meditate without being sure why. At this stage, your faith is somewhat intellectual, you have to convince yourself. But persevere with that initial calling; you will see for yourself that meditation really works, not only in developing calm and clarity, but also in dissolving your grasping and negative reactions and allowing yourself to let go.

As part of my daily duties during one three month retreat, I had to clean the communal bathroom. Every day I would go to the bathroom and find another nun there, washing herself. It was no use explaining to her that it would be easier for me if she washed at another time; she insisted that she had to wash there and then before a certain ceremony – no other time would do. This went on for more than two weeks: I would forget all about her till our moment of contact in the bathroom, and then I would become angry and resentful on seeing her there. One day, I opened the door; she was there, I was there and everything was fine. I saw then one of the effects of meditation. It dissolves the mind's subconscious hold on negative emotions and circumstances until suddenly the grasping is released. Then you can respond to life with ease and lightness. You realize that you can be free. Faith is no longer a matter of intellectual belief but grows organically with your experience.

Faith is the bedrock of practice. When you encounter difficulty and your vision is clouded, faith keeps you going. I once spent a month in a chalet in Switzerland. Every morning, I would open the window and look out at thick white fog. The chalet overlooked a lake just below the fog-line; I had only to walk uphill for two minutes for the fog to clear and the sky to be blue. In the light, the sun was obvious; it was warm, it illuminated everything. In the fog, I could not see a thing – but I knew the sun was real and nearby. This is faith. It inspires you to know that awakening is close, to trust in the potential of awakening when the clouds finally dissolve.

courage to continue

Faith directs you to the path; courage will give you the energy to continue. During my time in Korea, I heard many stories about respected monks and nuns, and how hard they practised. I was always inspired by these tales. There was a story of a monk who worked all day and meditated all night, for months on end. Many tried to join him but very few could follow his example. Master Kusan himself told us of a time when he felt he had to practise very hard in order to help a dying friend. He had promised his friend that in his stead he would become awakened within forty-five days. For the final two weeks, he meditated on tiptoe because he was afraid he would fall asleep and not attain awakening. On another occasion, I visited some nuns who were doing a three-year silent retreat. I was so impressed by their dedication and lightness; they managed to joke and make me laugh in the midst of their deep silence.

All these meditators were inspired by their own great courage. Nobody had forced them to do what they were doing. They were just so determined, so convinced of the merits of meditation, and with such faith in their own buddha-nature, that they gave the practice all they had. But for you who live in the West, in a busy modern world, what does it mean to have courage in meditation? You require courage to face your mental and emotional habits. It is easy to say that you do not have the time to meditate, that maybe you will do it tomorrow when you are less busy or at the weekend when you are less tired. You need the courage to meditate now, in this unrepeatable moment, whether tired or busy, sad or happy.

When you meditate, it is essential to have the courage to concentrate and enquire. As you sit quietly, doing nothing, you will very quickly be caught up in day-dreams, fantasies or worries. Courage bolsters your determination, reminds you to straighten your back and reaffirms your intention to be aware, to be awake, to be present. It enables you to break out of a

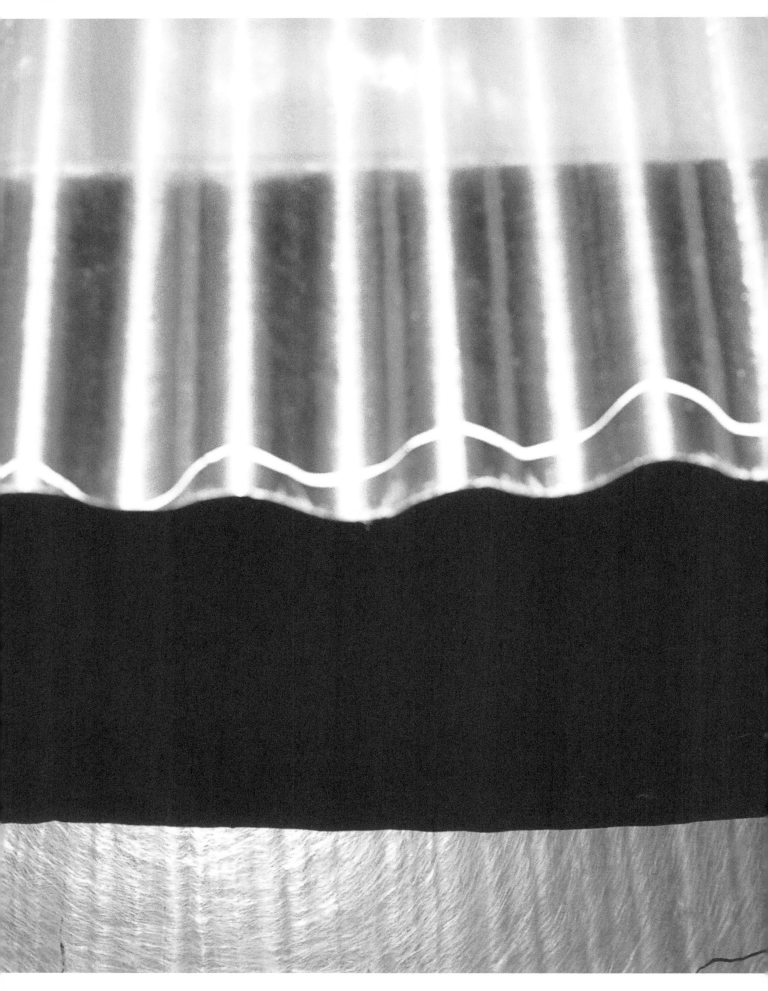

dull or lazy state of mind and to resist tempting thoughts. Going beyond your habits and patterns – the way of living that is easiest for you – requires a great deal of courage. When meditation is difficult, courage gives you the motivation to persevere. Master Kusan used to say that sometimes meditation is as easy as pushing a boat on ice, but at other times as difficult as dragging to a well a cow who does not want to drink. You need the courage to enquire, to question your habits, to step into the unknown. One of the paradoxes of meditation is that faith and enquiry are equally important. Faith alone can make you narrow-minded; enquiry alone can make you agitated. The practice of one helps and supports the practice of the other.

trust your experience

The Buddha put great emphasis on enquiry, on looking deeply into one's own experience. He was once asked by some villagers about the teachers who regularly passed through their village, advising them to follow this practice and that teaching. The Buddha told them to listen carefully and consider the meaning of what they heard. Did the teachings make sense? Could the villagers apply them? Would the practices help them? If applying a certain method made the villagers more skilful and wise, they should continue to practise it. If the results of a method were negative, they should discontinue it. The most important thing was to measure any teaching against the experience of their own lives. And this is what enquiry is about: considering one's own experience.

You should check out thoroughly any teacher or teaching – and also the way you practise. Is meditation helping you to become quieter and clearer? Is it helping you to be wiser and more compassionate? I once met a meditation teacher who told me a revealing tale about himself. An architect with a large office, he became interested in meditation and set aside a special corner of the building for that purpose. From time to time, he would announce that he was going to meditate and retire to this place. Then everybody would groan and dread his return because he would always be irritable and they had to put up with it, as he was the boss. When he realized that meditation seemed only to make him more angry, he started to observe how he meditated and saw that he was doing it all wrong. After that, he started to meditate properly and it finally did help him to become calmer and clearer.

I would like to give two more examples. One concerns a Western monk in Korea who needed to do four hours of meditation every day. Like a fix, he had to have his four hours – but not only that, when he sat in meditation, he required total silence. If someone in the room next door clinked a teaspoon in a cup, he would complain that it was too noisy to meditate. You must be careful not to become attached to meditation itself, or to its silence and stillness. Another Western monk came to our monastery in Korea to learn to meditate within a community. In Thailand, he used to go to an island and meditate on his own, with just a dog for company. There he could achieve a great state of stillness, but as soon as he came back to his large monastery he would get into difficulties. It is relatively easy to meditate on your own in a quiet place but you must be able to meditate under any circumstances, and bring creative awareness to your daily life and ordinary relationships.

p r a c

working with thought

Thoughts are very useful! They are the natural activity of the mind. However, they also have a tendency to proliferate, and to influence and dominate your character. Thoughts can become fixed mental habits that inhibit your natural wisdom and compassion. They can be as light as wispy clouds in a blue sky or as heavy as dark clouds before a storm. Meditation is a great opportunity to observe your thoughts. I have noticed three types of thoughts: intense, habitual and occupying.

intense thoughts

Intense thoughts generally arise because you have been shocked, because something painful has caught you unprepared. Thoughts that arise under the influence of shock and pain are often obsessive and repetitive. It is very difficult to deal with these thoughts because they are powerful and disturbing, and you can become lost in them. When you meditate, notice what is happening. Try to create space in your mind by telling yourself that repeating these thoughts is not helpful, that you are making the situation more intense. Just let them go! For a few minutes, relax in the meditation, in the silence, in the discipline of concentration and enquiry.

habitual thoughts

Mental habits are a groove in the mind into which you are inclined to fall over and over again.

day-dreaming

You might have a tendency to day-dream. Day-dreaming is characterized by a seductive, sticky feel. Like glue on your fingers, the more you try to get rid of it, the more it sticks everywhere. Day-dreaming often starts with 'if I had' and 'if I was' and then turns into a film where you are actor, director, producer and scriptwriter. In this film, life is wonderful. Everything goes according to your own plan without anybody's interference. You enjoy tweaking the dream here and there, rearranging this bit or that bit.

When I was in Korea, I used to spend days sitting in meditation day-dreaming that I was going to a hermitage to practise very hard, become awakened and save everybody. Then I realized I was not meditating but fantasizing about it. It was a total waste of time. You might have a tendency to day-dream about the perfect partner, house, child or job. Doing this too much leads to frustration because multidimensional reality will never fit into your one-dimensional dream. Concentrate on the breath and come back to reality, to the potential in this multifaceted moment.

going over the past

You might have a tendency to be obsessed by certain events in your past. Mulling over what has happened, you remember something somebody once told you or did that was painful. You repeat the story to yourself

t i c e

over and over again, feeling worse and worse. Then you move to the future and plot revenge, playing with various scenarios for maximum effect: 'She'll say this and I'll say that and then I'll get her . . .' But plotting revenge is not very compassionate! The past has gone. Can you learn from it? Can you let go of it instead of dragging it into the present and recreating pain?

fabrication stories

Another mental habit is to fabricate a story out of very little. This habit is often caused by fear and insecurity. A good example is the way people sometimes think when they are waiting for someone who is late. At nine o'clock your friend has not turned up: 'Well, I'll wait a little longer'. Ten past nine: 'He does not love me'. Twenty past nine: 'Nobody loves me'. Half-past nine: 'I hate the world!' When he does finally arrive, with a good reason for being late, you could be so upset by your fabrications that you are beyond reasoning. With enquiry, question whether it is really true that this person does not love you.

speculating

Another thought pattern is to speculate, to create elaborate intellectual constructions. You read this, hear that, you put this idea and that philosophy together, and bingo! you have developed the greatest idea of the century. Then you sit there, refining and repeating the speculation to yourself because you do

not want to lose your fantastic idea. But is it experiential wisdom? Is it something that you can apply and live? You have to be careful not to get lost in enticing constructions. Come back to the breath, to the experience of life in this moment as you sit in meditation. If you have truly had a great insight, it is there within you – you do not have to elaborate it *ad infinitum*.

planning

You might have a tendency to plan. Planning is very useful but has it become a habit? It is certainly a habit when you find yourself going over your plans for the hundredth time. By planning, we separate ourselves from the present and jump ahead in order to prevent any nasty surprises from happening. But life is unpredictable: a little planning is useful, too much is restrictive. Planning stops you from trusting in life and yourself. With awareness, returning to the object of concentration, come back to life in this moment. There is no need to plan anything for the next ten, twenty minutes – just be.

judging

You may have developed a habit of judging. Do you judge yourself, others, everything as good or bad, right or wrong? By judging, you set yourself a little above and apart from reality. You are constantly commenting instead of participating fully in whatever happens. You

47

need discrimination to know if something is hot or cold, salty or sweet. But when discrimination becomes a habit of judging it will weigh on you and your relationships. A judging mind is a heavy burden. How can you lighten it without judging the judging, which would be even more burdensome? Come back to the breath, the authenticity of this moment which is as it is: cold, hot, possibly pleasant, possibly unpleasant. Can you feel without attaching yourself to the sensation or to its quality?

calculating

Do you make a habit of counting and measuring? As you sit in meditation, you might be calculating how much money you have in the bank, or the size of your mortgage. You might be trying to count the breaths you have breathed since you were born. I know someone who would estimate how many miles he had covered during walking meditation. Calculation passes the time but is this really what you want to do in meditation? There is a time for counting and a time for letting it go.

procrastinating

Do you make a habit of complaining and procrastinating? You might tell yourself that you could meditate if only the room were more silent, that you could become a great meditator if only the instructions were better. You can cause yourself so much suffering with 'if only'. Now is the only moment, this is the only breath.

It is easier to notice and enquire into mental habits in meditation if you do not focus on them directly. Take another object of concentration, like the breath or a sensation within your body, and when you are distracted, gently notice the thought, naming it: 'day-dreaming' or 'planning' or 'calculating'. Do not spend

a long time describing the thought or explaining it to yourself. Just name it swiftly and come back to the object of concentration. In this way, the meditation will allow you to see your habits of mind without feeding them and increasing their hold on you. Do not be upset by your habits, just recognize them and, turning back to the meditation, rest again and again on the object of concentration. This will allow your mind to relax, to smooth out the groove of old habits and create a new groove of awareness, attention and gentleness.

occupying thoughts

The third type of thoughts are the light ones: the mechanical trains of thought where you start with Aunt Helga and ten minutes later find yourself thinking of New York, without being able to remember how you got from one to the other. You might spend your time making lists: what to take on holiday, what to cook for dinner, the clothes in your wardrobe, and so on. These are what I would call occupying thoughts.

Occupying thoughts do not have a great pull on your feelings or emotions. They just occupy the mind and provide something to think about. They are what the mind produces if it is left to roam at will. However, meditation requires a certain amount of discipline; you are cultivating concentration and enquiry. The aim is not just to sit there quietly without awareness. You are training the mind to become more alert in a soft but determined way. By noticing these light, occupying thoughts with enquiry, and returning to concentration, they become less sticky. If you want to think you can; if not, not. Thoughts become as light as bubbles and the mind is free and clear.

guided meditation: thoughts

- Find a comfortable posture, sitting on the floor or on a chair.

- Take as your object of concentration the breath as it passes through the nostrils.

- Observe the coolness of the air as you inhale and the warmth of the air as you exhale.

- Pay close attention to the sensation at the nostrils as the air passes through.

- Now notice carefully what takes you away from your object of concentration.

- Do you have a tendency to day-dream? Feel the enticing quality of these fantasies, note 'day-dream' and have the courage to come back to the breath.

- Do you make a habit of going obsessively over the past? Let it go, let it be. Noticing 'mulling over', return to the breath and the present.

- Are you fabricating a story out of fear or insecurity? Name it: 'fabricating' and come back to the breath. There is nothing to fear in this moment.

- Do you have a tendency to speculate? Note 'speculations'. Come back to the experience of the breath at the nostrils.

- Are you planning repeatedly? Name it: 'planning'. Do not jump ahead to the future, rest fully in the breath.

- If you are judging yourself or others, note 'judging'. Have faith in yourself in this moment, you are doing the best you can.

- Are you constantly calculating? Notice 'calculating'. Come back to the breath swiftly. You do not need to measure life. Appreciate it as it is.

- Watch out for trains of thought or lists. Let the mind rest on the breath, on life itself.

- Let the thoughts be as light as bubbles, gently coming and going.

- Come back to the breath, to awareness, to the world.

- Now open your eyes fully, stretch your back, relax your shoulders, and stand up with a different groove in your mind.

ethics

The three inseparable trainings of Buddhism are ethics, meditation and wisdom. Ethics provide the foundation of a meditative life; meditation leads to the blossoming of wisdom, and wisdom contributes to a more caring and ethical attitude.

ethics

the three trainings

There are three essential trainings in Buddhism: ethics, meditation and wisdom. They are inseparable and you need to cultivate all three simultaneously. Ethics make it easier to concentrate in meditation. Meditation supports the blossoming of wisdom. Wisdom and meditation allow ethics to arise naturally. Master Kusan used to say that ethics, meditation and wisdom are like the three legs of a tripod. If two or even one of the legs are broken, the tripod cannot be used properly.

Ethics in Buddhism does not mean blind rules and regulations. They do not exist to force you to do something, but to make you reflect on your motivations and actions. Since the aim of a Buddhist life is to diminish suffering, the root of Buddhist ethics is compassion and wisdom. You care for your own suffering and the suffering of others, and you understand that intentions and actions have consequences.

There are two essential components to an ethical attitude cultivated within the context of meditation. The first is respect that fosters restraint. You refrain from doing something that you know will cause suffering to yourself and others. You recognize that you are not alone in the world, that you share your environment with other people, animals and things, and that therefore there are limits to what you can do. You are encouraged not to cause harm, not to take what is not given, to be careful in your sexual behaviour, to be watchful of your speech and to be aware of the effects of intoxicants.

The second component of an ethical attitude is the cultivation of a positive approach to life. You consciously endeavour to think, speak and act with harmlessness, generosity, respect, honesty and clarity.

not harming

The first Buddhist ethic is not to kill. At its root is the recognition that every living thing has an equal right to his, her or its life. Everyone wants to be happy and not to suffer. Everyone shares the same air. Everyone has the buddha-nature. After I had been meditating for a while, I found I could no longer intentionally kill even a mosquito. I saw very clearly that all creatures had the same right to live as myself, and from then on I would catch mosquitoes with a glass and postcard

and release them outside. Once, someone asked Master Kusan if it would not be more compassionate to kill a butterfly that was stuck in a pot of jam than to let it struggle and die on its own. Master Kusan replied that to kill the butterfly would be less compassionate, because so long as the butterfly was alive it would want to continue living. You cannot become master of another's fate, even of a tiny insect's.

In general, one does not go around killing people. You might kill animals and insects, but do you really need to? Think about your motivation. Is there nothing else to eat? Are these animals dangerous? It is very easy to crush an ant because it is so small. Who cares? The ant cares! If the ant were an elephant, you would not be able to crush it just like that. So you might try not to kill anything if you can help it. But that does not mean becoming a nervous wreck, constantly checking you are not inadvertently crushing some insect. You need to be wise and reasonable when you try to be ethical. As you breathe, you kill many microscopic organisms. Worms and insects are destroyed during the cultivation of vegetables and cereals. Even if you are a vegetarian or a vegan, your diet will cause some harm. It is impossible to keep to an ethical position of absolute non-killing, but you can live with the intention of causing the least suffering possible.

The ancient Korean Zen master, Chinul, said that:

You have to know how to open and close the doors of the ethical guidelines.

Being too literal or too strict might not have the most beneficial result. People in a Buddhist centre in Canada once found a few cockroaches. As good Buddhists and meditators, they decided not to kill the cockroaches but to live with them and get rid of them by kind means such as taking them outside. However, as the months went by the number of cockroaches increased until there were so many that the centre was almost uninhabitable. Finally, the centre had to call in a specialized agency and hundreds of cockroaches were killed. In terms of life lost, it would have been much better just to have killed the first few cockroaches.

not wanting

The second ethic is not to take what is not given. One should not steal. One should be careful with other people's property (though it is so easy to forget to return borrowed books that they seem to fall into the category of not belonging to anyone in particular!). What this principle highlights is the power of wanting something, regardless of circumstances.

When I was living as a nun in Korea, I led a very simple life and had few possessions: just the essential items such as shoes, shirts, trousers and sweaters that were provided by the monastery. When I started to live in England as a layperson, I noticed how attracted I was to shoe shops and clothes shop – something seemed to be acting like a magnet between the shop windows and me! Yet during my ten years in Korea I had not experienced the urge to buy at all. A shop window was a shop window; the contents did not matter and I used to pass by without sparing them a glance.

In England, I reflected on the attraction of shopping. Walking up the high street with no particular agenda in mind, I would look in the shop windows and get the seductive feeling of 'that looks nice' followed by 'I want it!'. But my desire to acquire things was generally checked by the question of whether I could afford it. Nowadays, after fifteen years of living in England, acquiring and accumulating various objects, I ask myself whether I actually need another shirt. How many shirts does one person need at any one time?

On the surface, it might seem that, as long as you do not steal, being acquisitive does not hurt anything apart from your bank balance. But there is also the question of the environment and its limited resources to consider. How sustainable would it be to satisfy all of your desires all of the time? This ethical stance does not mean that you should neither need nor want material things, but rather that you should reflect on your relationship to them within a wider perspective.

From a personal, meditative point of view, consider how it feels when you covet something. There was a time when I would become fixated on a certain desirable object, a dress, for example. Since I lived in a small town, my desire could not be satisfied quickly, as I wanted not just any old dress but exactly the right one. For months I would think about what I wanted, plotting how to get it, trying on dress after dress until I finally acquired the object of my desire. However, satisfaction was brief and very soon another desirable object would loom on the horizon, and the plotting and obsession with an *idée fixe* would start again. When I finally became aware of this process, and how it took me over, the spell of material things began to lose its power. It is liberating to be able to notice that you are content with what you have in this very moment, notwithstanding new fashions and the constant

advertisement of enticing products. Satisfaction with what you have is a very peaceful and spacious feeling.

My husband and I recently had to furnish a new flat and so, every day, for ten days, we went shopping. Immediately afterwards, I went to teach a meditation retreat and it was only in the restfulness and peace of the retreat that I realized how exhausting those ten days had been, not only physically but also mentally and spiritually. If you are too focused on material things they dominate your life and you think constantly about nothing more than the right chair or table.

This experience reinforced my belief that you have to bring meditation to everyday life in order to dissipate your tendency to hold and consume. This does not mean that you have to renounce material things because they are dangerous. In themselves, things are not dangerous but simply as they are. It is how you approach things, how you consider them, how you relate to them and how you use them that will make the difference to how you live your life and how you feel inside.

sexual behaviour

The third ethic is to be careful about your sexual behaviour. You are encouraged to reflect on sexual desires and on your relationship to other people's bodies and feelings. You have a body, you feel, you have a heart and you have a sex. It is natural to want to express your body sexually. This act generally entails a partner; the principle here is to refrain from abusing and taking advantage of that person.

When you are becoming sexually involved with another person, you should reflect on what you are actually thinking and doing. Is your partner's happiness and satisfaction as important as yours? If you are thinking of being unfaithful, are you taking into consideration the pain that might be caused to all the people involved? When you are physically attracted to someone, can you look beyond his or her appearance and reach out to love the whole person? Ethics and meditation can help you to act with more wisdom and compassion, and to break out of self-centredness and selfish desires.

Sexual desire is intense and powerful. However, sex and love are integral to each other and cannot be separated. Love is a wonderful feeling but it is also daunting. You are very vulnerable when you are in love and a lot of emotion is brought to the surface. Your sexuality is a bodily expression of those feelings, and makes you even more vulnerable. So it is essential that your spiritual meditative life is not cut off from sexual feelings.

Meditation allows you to bring a deeper awareness and calm to relationships, which will enrich your love and sexuality. It also helps you dissipate the romantic myths and idealistic expectations that are a great obstacle to a healthy and confident loving relationship. For example, at the beginning of my relationship with my husband I kept day-dreaming about how we would become one and he would be able to read my mind. It was some time before it dawned on me that this was totally idealistic and unrealistic. I realized that telepathy was not actually necessary for us to understand and love each other!

communication

The fourth ethic is to refrain from lying. We should not spend time telling whopping great lies. We should also, as the Buddha explained in the *Dhammapada*, consider the harm that is caused by slandering other people, by speaking harshly and by indulging in idle gossip. Dishonesty is harmful to ourselves too because when we are dishonest we delude ourselves as well as others. Dishonesty complicates a situation and often leads to greater suffering.

slander

Slander is an interesting subject: where does healthy criticism stop and slander start? Notice how you are influenced by someone speaking critically of another person and how your own words can affect somebody else's opinion of another. I once had a friend round for lunch and she spent the whole time criticizing a common friend. I had no problem with that other person but, by the end of the lunch hour, I was feeling pretty bad about him. It is essential to remember that nobody can ever see the whole truth – one is generally blinded by one's own self-interest. By bad-mouthing somebody you serve that self-interest, colour other people's vision and encourage collusion.

harsh words

Speaking harshly comes out of impatience, frustration, anger and sometimes the desire to hurt or dominate. Meditation can be helpful in teaching you to be calmer, more composed and patient. It also enables you to recognize that harsh words do not help; on the contrary, they often make matters worse. We do not like it when we are spoken to harshly, either through someone's tone of voice or their choice of words. So it is not difficult to imagine how another person feels when he or she is on the receiving end of our own tempers.

idle gossip

Idle gossip is a difficult one for Buddhists because they love gossiping as much as the next person. What is gossip? There is a kind of idle talk that is useful as a social lubricant. There is also the kind of gossip that involves repeating scandalous tales and rumours, and talking behind someone else's back. I once heard of a meditator who decided to practise this injunction of not gossiping. He resolved that for three months he would not talk about anyone who was not present. He kept it up for the whole three months, and was amazed at how few conversations he could participate in. He estimated that his verbal output diminished by two-thirds! Although you do not want to become too precious about communication, this principle reminds you that speaking is another place where you can be creatively aware, kind and compassionate towards yourself and others.

avoiding intoxicants

The fifth ethic is to refrain from taking alcohol or any other intoxicant. There is a well-known Buddhist story about the unethical behaviour that might result from drinking alcohol:

A man, who had walked for many miles, was very thirsty and stopped at an inn. There was a pitcher on the table and, thinking it was water, he drank a few glasses to quench his thirst. However, it was laced with alcohol and the man became inebriated. When the owner's wife appeared, he seduced her. Then he felt hungry, so he killed the chicken

he had spotted in the courtyard. Finally, the owner
appeared and asked what on earth had happened to his
wife and chicken. The man replied that he had not done
anything, and continued on his way.

The moral of the story is that because of the alcohol the man manages, in a short space of time, to transgress the four other ethical guidelines too.

What is your motivation when you drink alcohol or take drugs? Are you trying to relax, forget, escape, feel different or have a good time? What are the physical effects of these substances and what are your consequent actions? Do you feel happy, sad, angry, spaced out, excited, anaesthetized? Do you become red in the face, do you forget to eat, do you hyperventilate?

There is a wonderful Japanese technique of meditation that is based on asking questions. The meditation consists of reflecting on sets of complementary questions for thirty minutes at a time. One set of questions is: 'What has your body done for you since you were born?' and 'What have you done for your body?' A friend of mine who was a smoker managed to stop for quite a while after a meditation retreat of this kind. She was suddenly struck by the fact that her body had given so much to her but she had done nothing in return, apart from fill its lungs with tar! Meditation is about being present to the moment, accepting what is in it and trying to work with that. Alcohol and drugs often take you away from that awareness.

Each of you is different and will want to apply these ethics differently according to your needs and circumstances.

The aim is not to restrict your freedom by putting you in an ethical prison but to provide guidelines for reflection and action that will help in your intention to cause the least suffering to yourself and others, and to achieve inner and outer peace.

three ethical attitudes

In Buddhism, there are three basic ways of interpreting ethics:

restraint

The first is to consider ethics in terms of restraint. This approach is most often emphasized in the Theravada tradition of Southeast Asia. In Theravadan Buddhism there are codified rules, which you follow strictly, avoiding any thought, speech or action that might break them. This way is the easiest because you can be sure you are not going to transgress. Restraint facilitates peace and concentration of mind. It can be represented by this verse proclaimed by the Buddha:

Not to commit evil
But to practise all good
And to keep the heart pure:
This is the teaching of the Buddha.

emptiness

Ethics can also be considered from the standpoint of emptiness. This attitude is most often emphasized in the Zen tradition, where it is said that any person, act or thing is in itself empty. (Emptiness is looked at in detail in the fifth chapter.) Nothing is purely good or bad as everything depends on intention, motivation and circumstances. There is no purity or impurity, no gain or loss. The seventh-century Zen master, Sengtsan, said:

Gain and loss, right and wrong:
Such thoughts must be finally abolished at once . . .
Do not dislike even the world of senses and ideas.
Indeed to accept them fully
Is identical with true enlightenment.

This perspective can give you freedom and space but only if you have no grasping or attachment. Sometimes people experience what is called *kensho* – Zen awakening – and think

that after such a transcendent experience they can do exactly what they want. However, what they often choose to do is drink, sleep around and take financial advantage of people. They might claim that they are beyond ethics because everything is empty anyway. But that is not true emptiness, as Master Sengtsan went on to say:

The great Way is not difficult
For those who have no preferences.
When love and hate are both absent
Everything becomes clear and undisguised . . .
Live neither in the entanglements of outer things
Nor in inner feelings of emptiness.

This perspective is more demanding than some people think. In order to achieve it, you have to go beyond yourself by letting go of all self-serving actions.

transformation

The third way of looking at ethics is found in the Tantric practices of the Tibetan tradition. Tantric Buddhism uses everything that is in life so nothing is discarded. Even what is impure can be transformed from within. For example, so-called 'impure' substances or acts like alcohol and sex are transformed into the ground of liberation. It is for this reason that alcohol is placed as one of the offerings on the Tibetan Buddha altar.

In the Tantric approach to ethics, unethical things are seen in terms of their energy. It is the energetic field of sex and alcohol, and not sex and alcohol themselves, that is used in practice. In this context, when you are having sex or drinking alcohol, you are totally free from attachment to sex or alcohol, and transmute their influence through your enlightened view. But very few people can actually do this – and you are told to perform many prostrations and other purification exercises before you can practise the ultimate Tantric view.

All these approaches are complementary. Sometimes it is best to restrain yourself in order not to do something harmful. At other times, it is important to go beyond good and bad. There is a story about a Japanese Zen teacher who goes shopping in town with his vegetarian Western disciple. The master orders a hamburger and the disciple a cheese sandwich. When the food arrives, the master takes the cheese sandwich and gives the hamburger to the disciple! And, finally, sometimes we have to be in the messiness of things in order to try to transform them from within.

Ethics arise naturally out of cultivating equally all of the three trainings. If you have certain aspirations and intentions, you will not have to continually restrain yourself or ponder endlessly on ethics because, intuitively, you will not think or act in a way that would be detrimental to yourself or others. And the more you practise the three trainings of ethics, meditation and wisdom, the more difficult it will become for you to act in a way that is contrary to an ethical, compassionate attitude.

My first inkling of this was when I went to change money in a bank in Korea. The teller gave me too much money and my initial reaction was: 'Great, one over the banking system!' However, almost immediately I remembered the teller and realized that he would get into trouble. So I retraced my steps and gave him the money back. I left the bank amazed by my behaviour, so uncharacteristic for a former anarchist! But my gain would have been his loss and I could not bring myself to deliberately cause harm to the teller.

p r a c

cultivating life

Being ethical when practising meditation means that on a day-to-day basis you try to cultivate life and help it grow. You reflect on the conditions that enhance existence and you actively participate in improving them in a practical way. You do not remain a bystander who thinks that he or she need only refrain from certain actions to be ethical. There are five qualities you can develop in your daily life: harmlessness, generosity, respect, honesty and clarity.

harmlessness

Harmlessness means reflecting on the kind of harm you might be causing to yourself and others. You can be quite hard on yourself, judging and putting yourself down for no reason, and you might do the same to other people. You can change these patterns by questioning their intrinsic reality. If you intend to cultivate harmlessness, you must deliberately be kinder to other people and to yourself.

Once, I was talking about harmlessness and a woman in the audience was struck for the first time by what the word truly meant. She used to have a habit of cutting her body; since the body was hers she had not seen her actions in terms of 'causing harm'. My remarks made her realize that even her actions directed at herself should also be seen in an ethical, compassionate context. It became part of her practice consciously

not to harm herself. We often develop coping mechanisms in childhood that later become habits and which can be damaging to our well-being. As adults, meditation and ethics help us realize that our coping mechanisms are no longer necessary.

generosity

Generosity is an important quality that is generally associated with money, although that is only a minor part of its meaning. How can you be more generous in your thought, speech and actions? The first step is to learn to give others – and yourself – the benefit of the doubt. It is so easy to be negative, expecting yourself to fail and others to be up to no good. If a small baby is crying, is your first reaction to think that he or she is doing it on purpose, just to be awkward and annoy you? No, you instantly react by asking yourself what the matter is and trying to soothe the child. In the same way, you could be open, spacious and generous in your relationships with yourself and other people.

respect

Respect is a vital quality. It sometimes gets lost in wanting to make one's way in the world, in grabbing what one can. I was once talking to a friend about relationships and he told me that his bottom line was t i c e

ethics

that his lover was there to satisfy his need and vice versa. This seemed to me a bleak vision of love.

The key to a loving relationship is respect. You are with a person because there is something you like about them, you enjoy their company, you are attracted to them. Yet very quickly you forget that they add something to your life and you want them there just to service your needs. This is so limiting. What can you do to make your relationship grow emotionally, sexually and practically? Each of you is different and has to find your own creative way to make love blossom – but small ways are often better than any grand gesture.

honesty

The source of words is the mind. We usually have a running commentary in our heads that greatly influences our communication. What are you actually telling yourself, from moment to moment? What kind of yarn are you spinning? Consider whether this inner dialogue is an honest reflection of what is going on. Are you deluding yourself in small or big ways?

Honesty can be cultivated by transforming your inner language. For example, you might think: 'I am no good' or 'they are no good'. Is this true? Have you really done something dreadful or have you just made a mistake? For some strange reason, people want to wallow in the idea of being either the best or the worst, and they will colour the truth rather than accept that there has been a mistake. What is true in this moment? How close can we get to the reality of our experiences?

clarity

Clarity of mind is characterized by spaciousness and brightness, and accompanied by stability. When can you see clearly? When are you befuddled and confused? Ask yourself what kind of conditions give rise to clarity or confusion. A smaller intake of intoxicants or none at all can help. But it is not only alcohol and drugs that confuse. Your mind can also be clouded by strong emotions, or anaesthetized by too much television-watching. We do not have a television at home and when I visit my mother and watch programmes with her, I notice that I can only take so much. After two or three hours of television-watching, my mind is mushy. Gossiping too can cloud the mind, as can overworking. Each of you must look at your particular circumstances and try to cultivate the clarity of your own mind so that it can shine more brightly for the benefit of yourself and other people.

the lying-down position

Meditation helps to make the mind clearer. You might think that you do not have enough time to do it,

63

but there is a way to meditate that can be easily managed on a daily basis – meditation in the lying-down position. You can lie down either on your side or on your back. The traditional posture is lying on the right side with the right arm bent and the head resting on the palm of the right hand; the left arm resting along the body. However, you might find it more comfortable to lie on your back, with a small pillow under your head. You can lie like this on your bed before going to sleep and when you wake up in the morning. If it is a warm day, you could go and lie down in the grass outside. Lying down can be the most relaxing meditation posture. The only thing you need to do is lie still and at ease.

meditation on sounds

Meditation on sounds can be very useful for cultivating openness and spaciousness, and for connecting with life. Concentrating only on the breath or the body, you can sometimes become too locked inside yourself. Listening to sounds is a wonderful meditation that opens you to the world around. Generally it is done in three stages: you start with sounds inside the body, then move to sounds nearby and then finally to sounds further away. Do not grasp at any particular sounds. Do not name them or make up stories about them. Do not discriminate – just listen to the sounds as they are.

I was once leading a retreat on a Sunday. We were all silently sitting in meditation when, suddenly, a neighbour put some music on: what sounded like the *Best of Rock and Roll* at full volume. For the next hour, forty of us tried to meditate while the Beatles sang 'Revolution'. It was deafening!

I thought this was a great exercise and later asked people how they had reacted. Some were very annoyed and said that they might as well have stayed at home, since what was the point in using a Sunday to meditate when it wasn't even silent? Others had experienced listening to the sounds as just sounds, no better or worse then my voice or the birds. It had been quite a revealing experience for them.

the lying-down position

guided meditation: sounds

- Find a comfortable posture, lying on a bed. Keep your eyes half-open but not fixed on anything.

- Be aware of your body lying there. Just feel it as it is and let it relax.

- Now pay attention to sounds in your body. Maybe you hear a gurgle, or a faint sigh.

- Do not create or imagine any sounds, just listen to the silence if you cannot hear anything.

- Now expand your awareness to sounds around you, inside the room.

- Do not grasp or reject any sounds. Just listen.

- Now expand your awareness to include all sounds: the birds, the wind, the traffic, a dog barking.

- Do not name the sounds, do not make up a story around the sounds. Just open your ears to the sounds of the world.

- If you become distracted, remember your intention to be present, to be aware, to meditate. Come back again and again to listening.

- Now look deeply into listening: where does sound stop and hearing start? Experience this seamless experience.

- Notice how ephemeral sounds are: they come and go, they do not remain exactly the same for very long.

- Open yourself to the music of the world without grasping anywhere.

- Rest in the quietness and clarity of this experience.

- Now stretch your body, move your limbs and gently get up, trying to maintain this quality of attention and non-grasping throughout the day.

wisdom

Wisdom does not mean knowledge but experiential understanding. Wisdom helps you to change radically your habits and perceptions, as you discover the constantly changing, interconnected nature of the whole of existence.

w i s d o m

Wisdom is the third Buddhist training. Wisdom, here, does not refer to an accumulation of knowledge but to an experiential understanding that enables you to make a radical shift in your perceptions and habits. The Buddha explained in the *Samyutta Nikaya* that there are three characteristics of existence – impermanence, unreliability and non-self or emptiness – and he taught that by knowing them one can develop wisdom. This knowing is not an intellectual exercise but a meditative one. You do not force yourself to believe in the three characteristics and revere them as sacred. On the contrary, you observe your experience from moment to moment, and realize that impermanence, unreliability and emptiness are fundamental to your whole existence.

impermanence

It is obvious that day follows night, that the seasons come and go, that flowers stay fresh only for a few days. However, we generally live as if things, people and events are permanent. Yet it is extremely difficult for you or anything else to stay exactly the same for twenty-four hours, let alone day in, day out. Impermanence has two aspects: death and change.

death

Death is a given. You are born to die. Looking around, you can see that things come into being, stay for a while and then pass away. Some are ephemeral, like flowers and insects, others have a longer life span, like humans, elephants and oceans. When I was a nun, impermanence was my Buddhist motto. If I broke a vase, I would say: 'Oh, it does not matter, all things are impermanent.' This was a very superficial understanding of impermanence, just a way of escaping from the exigencies of reality.

It was not until I saw my father breathe his last breath and die that I truly understood impermanence. In that instant, I realized that I was mortal and so were my family and friends, and that anyone who was alive would one day die. This experience had the immediate effect of making life seem more precious. I felt so much more compassion and spaciousness for my mother and my sisters because I realized that they too could die at any moment. When I realized that each of their lives rests on a single breath, I could no longer take them for granted. The paradox of death is that it makes you more conscious of life.

We generally live as if we will carry on for many more years; at least long enough to pay off the mortgage and enjoy a pension. There is a certain feeling of invincibility – until death happens to you, it is always someone else who dies. You assume that people will be around for a lot longer than they might so unconsciously you feel you can afford not to try too hard with them. Being unkind or neglectful does not matter, there will always be another day to improve matters. But there might not be! Intimate knowledge of the possibility of death makes you live more fully, more intensely, because you know that each minute is unrepeatable.

Death demonstrates what is essential. You realize that an argument over cleaning is a small, irrelevant matter, which does not define who the other person is or who you are. When you are in direct contact with the possibility of death, you can be more spacious about human foibles – though if someone is unkind or treacherous, you will not hesitate to deal with the matter straight away. Death gives rise to gratitude for life, for your potential. It makes you realize that it is amazing to be alive – to be breathing, seeing and feeling. You become present to every breath, to every nuance of life. You become more caring without being attached or fearful. Less heedless and unprepared, you accept life on its own terms.

A few months before Master Kusan died, we went for a walk. As we were resting for a few minutes, he looked at me piercingly and said: 'We do not know how we will be when confronted with death, so we have to prepare ourselves. In order not to be frightened and not to despair in the face of death, we need to meditate assiduously so that we will be ready whenever it comes.'

I found his words very humbling. Master Kusan had experienced three awakenings but even he did not know what would happen when he died. So he continuously prepared himself for death, at the same time enjoying, moment by moment, all the life he had left. Until his last days, though he was half-paralysed by a stroke, he asked to be sat in the meditation posture so that he could meditate formally.

change

The second aspect of impermanence is change. When Buddhists talk about impermanence they are not being pessimistic – on the contrary, impermanence is a treasure house of possibilities. Impermanence means that at any moment there is potential for change; you are not doomed to be stuck in the same habits for ever. It is liberating to know that the possibility for change and improvement exists.

I used to have a habit of locking my car keys inside the car, and would have to phone my husband Stephen to rescue me. After several such occasions, he said in exasperation: 'You always lock your keys in the car!' For a moment I had a dreadful vision of always doing the same thing – day after day, year after year. Then I looked into what might cause the situation and saw that it usually only happened after I had had difficulty parking in a tight place. Thereafter, in these situations, I have made a point of grabbing the keys before getting out of the car, and I have not locked them in since.

unreliability

We are quite happy for difficult feelings, sensations and events to be impermanent. Less pleasing is when it is joy, happiness, peace, wealth and health that change. Therefore, the second characteristic of existence is unreliability. There is nothing to rely on because everything changes. Yet, we are still addicted to the hope that one day something will provide us with everlasting happiness. So we try to get things right, seeking out a loving partner, perfect children, a fulfilling job, a beautiful house, interesting experiences – but none of these ever give more than fleeting happiness. You have to be careful with what you expect because nowadays people feel it is their right, and even their duty, to be happy, and if you are not you might feel like a failure. Understanding unreliability makes you see that happiness depends on both inner and outer conditions and cannot be guaranteed. You must not aggravate your unhappiness by telling yourself that you have to be happy at all times. Instead, look with enquiry at what is actually happening.

For example, I recently went on holiday to a beautiful and sunny island in the Canaries. I think it is great to be in a nice place where the sun shines, but the representative from our travel company, who had been there for twenty years, told us how much she missed the Scottish fog! We are rarely contented with our conditions for long. Often, something seems to be missing because peace and happiness do not reside in outside conditions, be they where we are or what we own, but in the heart. Acceptance of the unreliability of not just things but also of feelings and emotions is the key to contentment. It does not mean becoming fatalistic but being creative and flexible with what you have. Unreliability means that you can care for people deeply but should not grasp at them or try to fix them, because they cannot stay the same for very long.

One aspect of unreliability is suffering. We often suffer because things are unreliable: the car breaks down, you are ill in hospital. You can alleviate suffering if you understand that it is reinforced by your denying, fighting and complaining about the unreliability of things. When I was in Korea, I became quite ill with stomach pains. I went around moaning, wallowing in self-pity. The first thought of self-pity: 'Why me?' implies that I would not have minded somebody else taking on my pain – not very compassionate, to say the least! Finally, I looked at my body and mind meditatively, and realized that all along I had been experiencing the very suffering that the Buddha talked about. Nobody was immune from it, not even Buddhist meditators! Realizing that I had to live with the unreliability of the body allowed me to drop my burden of self-pity and opened my eyes to awareness. Once I had thought about the conditions that were most likely to give rise to stomach pains, I became quite a good friend to my stomach.

Having always been healthy myself, I used to be disparaging about those who were ill. At the time, it was popular to think that illness was all in the mind. If people were sick, I would tell them not to be so weak and to pull themselves together. Only after I had experienced for myself the physical dimension of suffering could I realize how painful it was. From then on, I empathized with others in pain. I could reach out to them and be with them in their suffering. One of the worst aspects of illness is that only the sufferer can feel it; nobody else can share the pain. Illness and pain are very isolating. All you can do to help is be there and respond to the suffering with compassion. You need to know, to accept suffering in order to deal with it appropriately.

And this knowledge, this wisdom about suffering will give rise to compassion.

A great source of suffering is identification with it. Once, Master Kusan had a huge boil on his foot. Everybody suggested trying this or that remedy but they only made the boil worse. One day, I met Master Kusan crossing the wide courtyard alone, without anyone to help him. I was very concerned about his foot and his pain, but he told me: 'The foot is painful but I am fine.' He was acknowledging that there was pain but also telling me that he was not identifying with it. This was just the way his foot was at that moment; according to circumstances the situation would change.

emptiness

The third characteristic of existence is emptiness or non-self. Emptiness does not mean that nothing exists or that everything is empty. The aim of meditation is not to push yourself into an empty void. Emptiness actually means being empty of a separate, concrete, autonomously-produced self. However, our tendency is to experience things as independent entities and we often imagine that inside everything and everyone there is an unchanging, solid and fixed kernel. Let's take a chair, for example. Inside that chair there is no kernel inscribed 'chair'. The chair only becomes a chair when all its parts – four legs, a seat and a back – are combined in the right way. Without a back, the chair is a stool. Without a seat, it is not a chair.

The 'chairness' of the chair is not in the legs, the seat or the back. The chair is empty of existing separately from its parts.

Furthermore, no specific characteristic resides in the chair, even if you attribute one. If you are very tired, it is a 'nice' chair to rest in. If you bump into it in a hurry, it is a 'bad' chair that is in the way. The quality of the chair is not intrinsic but depends on many different conditions: the way it is made, how old it is, where it is placed, how you relate to it. You can also look into the parts that make up the chair, they too are neither fixed nor independent. Take the legs, for example. The legs are made of wood. The wood comes from a tree. The tree needs a seed, rain, earth and the sun to grow. Each of these is not the tree itself but an element that contributed to the tree's existence. This example shows clearly that things are not finite, limited and independent. Instead, everything is connected by endless possibilities and relationships.

non-self

There is no independently existing self. If you look into yourself, you will not be able to find a kernel that is 'you'. You are the result of various conditions coming together: your physical body, your mind, your parents' genes and influence, the culture and society in which you have been raised, the food you eat, the air you breathe, the experiences you had and are having, and so on and so forth. All these components are part of you but you are not reducible to any one. In this way, you are a flow of conditions.

Language can influence you in affirming the notion of a separate self. You think: 'I am doing this', 'This is my house'. You can question and weaken this tendency by using non-fixing terms and think of yourself as a 'flow of conditions' doing this or that. Every morning, you might go to the park and sit in the same place on the same bench. Very quickly it becomes *your* place on *your* bench. If someone else sits there, you get upset. But the place never was yours, even when you were sitting there. The more you identify with 'me' and 'mine', the more you limit yourself and cause yourself pain.

Believing in the non-existent self would not matter too much if we did not attribute fixed qualities to things. I used to hate rhubarb because I found it sour and acidic. Every spring, in the British Buddhist community where I used to live, the other members would get excited about eating rhubarb pie. This would make me think that there must be something wrong with them. Rhubarb was bad; if they liked rhubarb they must be bad too. With meditative training and better recipes, I learnt to make peace with rhubarb and rhubarb eaters.

I have a friend who used to be a monk in Thailand. As a monk, he had to beg for food to eat, and he had to accept anything that was put in his bowl. People would often give him these crunchy, nutty red nuggets, which he used to like – until he found out that they were actually fried red ants. After that discovery, he could not eat them any more. The way you relate to anything depends very much on the way you approach it.

When you look at yourself, you have a strange feeling that inside you must be a kernel called 'Martine', or 'Stephen', or 'Paul' or 'Laura', that defines you for all time and makes you separate from other people. But reflect on the changes that have happened over your lifetime, as you have grown from a helpless baby to a young child to an adult. There are as many changes in a human lifetime as between a caterpillar and its manifestation as a butterfly. You have come into being through your many parts. As these parts change and expand, so you too change and expand. Physically, mentally and emotionally, every human being changes continuously in many different ways.

Sometimes the changes are slow, at other times they are fast. Whenever I wash my hair and observe a few more grey hairs, I am made very much aware of the pace of change. Even in the space of one day you can get up lively and glowing and by the evening be bedraggled and exhausted. If you identify with the glowing person, you will suffer when the glow has gone; if you identify with the tired person, you will feel even more weary and hopeless. Notice that your perception of yourself depends on inner and outer conditions. If you see these conditions with wisdom, clearly and lightly, life will become like a dance and you will flow lightly through its different situations.

Sometimes you may feel as lonely as if you had no connection to anything or anyone in the whole world. With meditative wisdom, look into your experience of this very moment. Breathing keeps you alive; you are made of breathing. There are no borders in the space around you so you are actually breathing the same air as the people and the animals nearby. Their air goes into your lungs and your air goes into their lungs. How could you be more intimate than this with another human being? Through the breath, you are connected to the whole of humanity. The trees give out oxygen, so you are sharing air with them too. You are interconnected with the whole world.

break out of your box!

When I reflect on the nature of 'self', the image that comes to mind is of living in a large, solid box. To make yourself feel better, you accumulate bits and pieces in every corner of your box. And at the same time, you build the walls higher and higher, sturdier and sturdier, because you believe that you have to protect the small, fixed kernel of yourself from the outside. You stand in the box and look out over its parapet at the world. If the walls are low enough, you can step over them

to meet others. But truly there is no kernel, no box, no corners and no walls. You can be free if you drop this limiting image of the self as a separate, fixed entity. Meditation will help you let go of the walls and the fear as you see that there is nothing to defend and that no one is attacking you.

Yet when you look within yourself, you might still feel something pricking you inside. As if your heart were a pincushion, all the painful words you have ever heard seem to stick there like pins. From time to time you remember something hurtful that someone once said to you, and a pin draws blood. But look at a painful word — what is it? As soon as it is uttered, it is gone. A word is empty of inherent existence, why would you want to make it more real than it is? When you hear a word, consider whether it has any relevance to the situation at hand but do not store it. In reality, there is no pincushion, no pins and nothing for them to stick to.

the intricate web of life

There is no self but there is a relative sense of self. This sense of a relative or conditional self is necessary to function in the world, and you contribute to its healthy state by meditating. What makes you different from other people is the fact that the conditions — the memories, upbringing and attributes — that form this relative self, are different from someone else's. The self only becomes a problem if you take it to be permanent, unchanging and self-produced.

By reinforcing individualism, modern society actually accentuates feelings of being isolated, lonely and lost. Cultivating wisdom makes you realize that you are part of an intricate web of relationships, irremediably connected to everything through the breath, through the food that you eat. Everything you feel, think and do is dependent on something else and, in turn, you influence everything around you. This is what in Buddhism is called interdependence. Emptiness means that everything is connected and interdependent. The thirteenth-century Japanese Zen master, Dogen, expressed this in a poem:

The way of the Buddha
Is to know yourself.
To know yourself
Is to forget yourself.
To forget yourself
Is to be enlightened by all things.

You develop your own wisdom through understanding and insight into your experience. If you reflect on what is beneficial and what is not, on what causes suffering and what does not, you can act confidently upon that knowledge. You need to look behind your assumptions about yourself, other people and the world. The liberating thing about wisdom is that it also means accepting that sometimes you do not know anything. Wisdom is about knowing and unknowing in equal parts.

prac

effortless effort

When you are on the meditative path, you need endurance to overcome deeply ingrained habits. Intellectually, you may understand impermanence, unreliability and emptiness, but it is hard for this understanding to become experiential reality. For habits to dissolve, you have to meditate and notice the three characteristics over and over again. Sometimes you might have a sudden insight but this will quickly be obscured, and you will go back to acting out of the old habits of fear and separation. Today, we are so used to technology and rapid progress that it is hard to endure setbacks. Press a switch and the light comes on; turn on the tap and water flows. We are used to things being easy and comfortable, and it is upsetting if they are not.

Maybe you have a tendency to procrastinate. You do not feel too good today, the atmosphere is not right, you think it might be better to meditate tomorrow or the day after. But you need to practise right now, in this moment, with conditions as they are. Master Kusan would use the analogy of ice in winter. If the sun shines for a day, the ice does not melt. But if the sun shines for many days, the ice melts and then there is water for washing and cleaning. In the same way, if we do not practise regularly and assiduously we will not be able to break through our patterns and habits to awakening.

Endurance is not grim, you do not need to grit your teeth. Having endurance only requires determination.

It helps you bring energy and enthusiasm to the practice. Remind yourself that meditation and wisdom are beneficial and also fun to cultivate. Nobody is forcing you to meditate. Your habits have hardened for twenty or thirty years, it is going to take more than a week or two to weaken them. Meditation is a lifelong process of understanding, loosening and unfolding. You must be careful not to expect quick results; things move in their own way. Help your flow of conditions by bringing willingness and attention to this task of meditating and cultivating wisdom.

You need to put much effort into meditation, without becoming attached to your effort. Bring your understanding of the three characteristics to endurance and effort as well. Try with dedication but without expectations; do not judge or blackmail yourself. Be intent and attentive without grasping at any result. This is cultivating effortless effort – trying not too much and not too little but just enough. Try to tune your effort like a guitar. If the strings are too tight, they will break. If they are too loose, the guitar cannot be played properly. You must tune the strings and tighten them just so. It is the same with the practice of meditation; try gently without forcing yourself. Effortless effort is characterized by a light but steady intention that is energized with inspiration.

t i c e

guided meditation: death

- Find a quiet and undisturbed space. Sit in a comfortable but firm position: your back straight, your shoulders relaxed and open.

- Rest your attention on the breath. In this moment, your life rests upon a single breath.

- Appreciate the potential for change that each breath is giving you.

- Now rest your attention on death. You are born and then one day you die.

- Now reflect on the fact that death is certain. Recollect all the people that you know personally, or have heard about, who have died.

- Realize that nobody lives for ever. At some point all beings die.

- Now reflect on the fact that the time of death is uncertain. Recollect the various ages at which people you knew died – as a baby, as a youth, as a middle-aged person, as an old person.

- People die at all ages and in all manner of circumstances. You never know when you are going to die.

- Since death is certain but the time of death is uncertain, what is the most important thing for you to do at this moment?

- Reflect on what is essential and meaningful for you. What are you good at? What do you enjoy? What do you want to do?

- In what way can you realize the potential that birth gave you?

- Now – hearing, feeling, smelling, sensing and thinking – appreciate the life you have in this moment. Be present to life in the light of death.

- Breathing deeply a few times, experience your body fully and, gently getting up, embrace life and death.

compassion

Compassion is an essential part of a
meditative approach to life — meditation
does not mean self-absorption but openness
and connection to others. Wise compassion
goes beyond appearances to respond to
the potential in us all.

compassion

creative compassion

Compassion is an essential component of the Buddhist way of life. It is at the heart of meditation because meditation is not about self-absorption but, on the contrary, leads to openness and connection with others. However, your compassion is as much for yourself as for other people — in order to feel compassion, openness and love towards others you have to feel them for yourself. In Buddhism, compassion and wisdom are the two sides of the same coin. Compassion by itself can be mushy and misguided; wisdom by itself can be dry. Expressed together, compassion and wisdom contribute to a more generous life.

At the root of creative and skilful compassion is an understanding of the three characteristics of existence — impermanence, unreliability and emptiness. For example, awareness of death makes you realize that life is precious and fleeting, which gives rise to compassion for yourself and others. To know that everyone has the potential to learn makes you more spacious and supportive, and allows you to let others change in their own way and at their own pace. When I read the beautiful and poetic memoir, *Under the Eye of the Clock*, by the Irish writer Christopher Nolan, I was struck by the compassion and wisdom of his parents, who raised him with great love and creativity. They helped their son to realize his potential, despite his severe disability. Compassion and wisdom go beyond appearances to respond to the potential in us all.

Suffering also awakens compassion. Because you recognize that suffering is painful, you want to relieve it. You can empathize with the suffering of others, feeling their pain as your own, because we are all part of the same life and share the same air. Shantideva, an eighth-century Indian monk, compared the whole of life to a single body. When your foot hurts, your hand immediately reaches out to relieve the pain — not because your hand can feel the pain but because there is a shared sense of suffering.

A compassionate response to suffering can push you beyond your fears and limitations. I was once hurt deeply by a friend, which made me very careful around him. However, my reluctance to have much to do with him disappeared when he became very ill; I just responded to the person in pain and spent a lot of time helping him. The Dalai Lama often makes

the point that all beings are the same, in so far as they all want happiness and to be free from suffering. By feeling for one another, you realize that you are not so different and not such strangers after all.

misguided compassion

Compassion means feeling with and feeling for. It is not passive, it is an active quality that only becomes truly creative when accompanied by wisdom. You must be careful and reflective when you are responding with compassion.

self-serving compassion

In Korea, there is a tradition of sharing food, and one rarely eats alone. Once, I was travelling on a bus and, being hungry, bought some peanuts. I felt I could not eat them on my own and had to share them with somebody. Looking around for a likely recipient, I found a very small boy with his mother. I gave him some nuts and within five minutes there was chaos: there were nuts all over the place. This was what I would call self-serving compassion: doing something to make yourself feel good without responding to a specific need. The incident taught me not to forget to bring wisdom to my compassion.

By cultivating concentration and enquiry, your mind becomes more spacious, which helps you to respond appropriately, from the right motives. Misguided compassion actually creates more suffering. One wrong motive is assuming that what is good for me is also good for you. This is not necessarily true. Throughout history, much suffering has been imposed on people who are forced to take on the habits, culture and religion of their oppressors. Yet the oppressors have always argued that what they are imposing is good for these people, even that they are saving them from themselves. This type of argument is generally self-serving. Good intentions and misguided ideas are a dangerous mixture. Real compassion starts from empathy, from actually imagining yourself in someone else's shoes and truly listening to their needs.

A friend of mine was once going through a bad patch. I asked what I could do to help and she suggested I start visiting her mother, who was in an old people's home. Before my first visit, I imagined it would be a great opportunity for me to tell this elderly woman about Buddhist ideas, thinking that surely she would benefit from hearing about death and impermanence. However, when I met her it was obviously not one of her good days. She kept seeing huge insects in the room and she was terribly frightened. After that, the main thing I did during my visits was distract her and remind her of the good things she had enjoyed. To be able to do that I had to ask about her life and interests, and get to know her. Whenever she became anxious, I would bring the conversation back to cricket or country walks, to jam or pruning roses; no mention of death or impermanence, which would have been totally inappropriate. What she liked most about my visiting her was that I could sit quietly with her, which she found very restful. Compassion asks you to be open to the present conditions and respond to them wisely.

superior compassion

You have to be careful not to fall into what I call superior compassion. This happens when you feel that you are doing people a great favour by helping them. Actually, you should be grateful to them for allowing you to be compassionate. Thanks to the people you help, you can open your heart; you would not be able to actively express compassion if they were not there. In compassion, you are equal; both parties gain from the exchange. And, at another level, there is no gaining – just a natural connection and response. Sometimes you are in need, sometimes other people are in need.

your limitations

When you offer compassion, consider your circumstances and limitations wisely. You have to take care of yourself too. You might want to help but cannot because you are exhausted or ill. At other times, you might take on too much and your actions will be negative because you are too busy to reflect properly. Sometimes, the urgency of a situation impels you to give beyond your capacity, but the pain of certain situations can be overwhelming and you might not be able to sustain such great effort for long. Being compassionate might also put you in a dangerous situation: not everybody is able to cope with that. Acknowledging that some people have a greater capacity for compassion than others does not mean that you cannot be creatively compassionate in your own way, within your own set of circumstances.

It is wonderful when you can help change a situation for the better. However, at times you cannot change anything and the only thing you can do is be there. When you are compassionate, it is easy to become disheartened and uninterested if things do not move forward. Compassion asks you to be steady and patient, and not to expect any result. Compassion should not necessarily be based on a potential

outcome, it requires humility. At times, there is no easy answer to find, even with the help of wisdom.

giving well

One of the active elements of compassion is giving. The Buddha was very clear about giving. He said that there are four types of people: those who give only to others, those who give only to themselves, those who give to neither and those who give to both themselves and others. He encouraged people to cultivate the fourth option.

material giving

When you give material things like money, goods or services, what is your intention? Often the subtext is that you expect something in return – if not something concrete, at least gratitude. Notice if you are offended when you give something and are not thanked for it. Sometimes you might even give a small something in the hope of getting a bigger something in return. True giving does not come with strings attached.

True compassionate giving is not about bargaining or profit. Compassionate giving is without expectation. Master Kusan used to say it is like giving a dirty mop. You would not expect a great or even a reasonable return on a dirty mop, you would just be grateful that someone is taking it away. However precious your gift, give it without expectation and with wisdom. What is needed? What can you give?

meditative giving

You can also give spiritually – meditatively – but you have to be careful about trying to convert people. The Buddha

was very clear about this. If somebody asks you about meditation or the teachings, you should respond. If no one is interested, let it be. You need to practise yourself, put the meditation into action and have an influence through the changes you make in your own life. The way you live is more important than what you say. It is easy to talk about having compassion for all beings, but what about your neighbour? Is he or she included in 'all beings'? You must be careful not to moralize. People usually find it unpleasant and will watch to see that you live up to what you preach.

One essential thing you can give to yourself and to other people is time. In the language of modern aphorisms, 'time is money'. We can be quite stingy with 'our' time. Too busy to give compassion, we do not always feel we have the time to stop and respond. Once, Master Kusan was going to an important meeting in another town. His car had arrived and he was being rushed along by the excited administrators, who were pressing him to leave in good time. I just happened to pass by and, as was the custom, bowed to him and wished him a good journey. He stopped to acknowledge my greeting and then asked if a monk, called Popchon, still had the flu. I said he had, so Master Kusan went back to his room to get some orange juice for monk Popchon. What impressed me is that he did not grasp at the busyness around him but found the space and time to stop, be kind and concerned, and respond in a practical way.

receiving well

Receiving is also part of compassion but comes less easily than giving. Notice, when someone praises or thanks you, if you push the compliment away, saying that what you did was nothing. When someone gives something to you it is important to accept it graciously. However, you must be careful about feeling indebted. You might receive something and straight away be thinking about what you should give in return. Just give and receive, nothing else is needed. Whatever comes next is something different and will engender its own set of giving and receiving circumstances. Giving and receiving – compassion back and forth – is enough in itself.

Sometimes you are not given exactly what you want. How do you receive it skilfully? At other times, you are given something you do not want at all. How can you take it kindly? How can you refuse skilfully? Receiving apologies can also be a lesson in compassion. You might feel vindicated and want the other person to grovel. Instead, can you just listen and accept the apology with kindness, compassion and wisdom?

It is easy to have compassion for people who are downtrodden and far away, for cuddly animals or defenceless babies. But you also need to show compassion towards difficult people, who might not be nice to you, who are grumpy, dissatisfied and gloomy. Compassion does not mean only responding to people who fit your criteria of being worthy of compassion. It also means helping people who do not fit anywhere, who do not do what they are supposed to do. Look beyond what bothers you about them. Like yourself, they want to be happy and not suffer. Can you respond to them at a basic human level? You might not be able to help them in a practical way but can you give them time and space in your mind, in your life? People who are happy are generally easy to be with. People who are suffering, anxious and afraid are often difficult, because their lives are difficult. Remember this, when you deal with them. Be kind and considerate, and honour their humanity and potential.

your family

Compassion needs to be especially creative when it comes to family relationships. You want your family to be more loving, more understanding, more on your wavelength – to be different from what they are. There are many expectations on all sides. How can you be more compassionate towards yourself, your parents and your siblings in the context of your particular family history? Remember that these people are human beings just like yourself, with joys and suffering, strengths and limitations. You also have to realize that the older your parents become, the less likely they are to change.

Can you be with your family in a different way? Can you be less confrontational and more accepting, without condoning whatever you disagree with? The most compassionate way to relate to parents is at an ordinary level, talking about their lives. What positive things do they feel connected to? In difficult situations, you might need to be creatively distractive and talk about something light and non-confrontational. Then, maybe, from these ordinary conversations a softer link can be created human being to human being – not in the past or the future but in the present moment.

rejoicing with others

Compassion also means rejoicing in someone else's happiness. What do you do when a friend tells you a piece of good news?

Perhaps you quickly deflate them by finding drawbacks in what they are pleased about. If so, they might wonder if you are truly their friend. Why put a damper on someone's happiness? Maybe you are unconsciously afraid that there is only a certain amount of happiness in the world. If someone else gets a big piece of the pie, you suspect that you are going to get a much smaller piece. But that is not how it works. Happiness and joy are self-perpetuating, they engender more happiness and joy. If you wholeheartedly rejoice with someone else, your happiness will be that much greater. You will not lose out, you will gain.

equanimity in compassion

It is essential to bring equanimity to compassion. You might sometimes feel overwhelmed by the suffering of the world but you have to be careful not to grasp at pain. Be aware of it but do not indulge the feeling. Make sure that your compassion does not descend into sympathetic self-pity. Self-pity is a heavy, very sticky emotion connected to many mental and emotional habits. The challenge and the paradox of compassion is to be fully involved and responsive without being so coloured by circumstances that you lose yourself. However terrible pain and suffering are, they are not the only conditions of life. Pain and suffering, peace and joy coexist in your own flow of conditions and in the flow of conditions of other people.

p r a c

four heavenly abodes

The four heavenly abodes – loving-kindness, compassion, sympathetic joy and equanimity – are qualities that are actively cultivated in meditation. You concentrate by repeating a verse connected to each quality and you enquire by visualizing yourself and other people in the light of each quality. As you meditate, you see others as human beings just like yourself – suffering and wanting to be happy – and you consciously wish them well. A basic formula to repeat in meditation is:

May you be happy.
May you be at peace.
May you be free from suffering.

loving-kindness

You usually start by meditating on loving-kindness. The Buddha himself recognized loving-kindness as an antidote to fear. Once, some monks who were meditating deep in the forest came to him for advice about how to deal with fear. They were afraid of being alone in the forest, of the animals there, of other people, of the dark. The Buddha suggested they practise loving-kindness meditation, so that by opening their hearts to the world and seeing it as benign, they would dissolve their fears.

Loving-kindness is about benevolence, about wishing happiness to yourself and other people. It requires you to connect with yourself and to recognize and acknowledge others for what they are. Love is an outward movement from the heart that impels you to break out of narrow self-centredness and open up to the whole world. Loving-kindness reminds you that acceptance is at the root of love. It is about gratitude for life, for your own existence and for other people, without whom you would be alone.

In loving-kindness meditation, you begin by visualizing yourself and wishing yourself well. As you do so, repeat this verse several times in silence:

May I be healthy.
May I be happy.
May I be at peace.

Then the meditation moves on to the people who live near you. Taking each person in turn, you visualize them, wish them well and silently repeat the verse, using 'you' instead of 'I'. After this, the meditation is widened to send love to the animals, trees and plants in your vicinity, and you wish them well too. Then your awareness is opened to the people you get on with, the people you love and the people you feel neutral towards, like the ticket collector, a shopkeeper, a neighbour, or a passer-by. Finally, you move to the people you do not like very much and wish them well too.

If there is time, the loving-kindness meditation can be continued by opening your heart to more and more people: the inhabitants of a certain town, a country, the whole world. The meditation is finished by repeating the verse, using 'all beings' instead of 'I' or 'you'.

You may find that after this meditation you feel open and warm but you must be careful not to try to force yourself to create these feelings. The loving-kindness meditation is a powerful concentration and enquiry exercise. It redirects your intention, thoughts and feelings towards openness and kindness.

compassion

The second quality to meditate on is compassion. Compassion means having empathy with your own suffering and the suffering of others. You acknowledge that suffering exists, is painful and can lead to great isolation. Nobody can truly feel the pain of someone else, but you can try to empathize. Stop and listen to other people's problems, be with their suffering, break through their isolation. The specific verse for this meditation is:

May you be free from pain.
May you be free from sorrow.
May you be free from danger.

As in loving-kindness meditation, start with compassion for yourself. Then move to people nearby and then all the living things in your vicinity. Later, consider friends, then the people you feel neutral towards. Finally, extend your compassion to people you see as your enemies, realizing through this meditation that they are ordinary human beings, suffering just like you do. Finally, end the compassion meditation by opening your heart to all beings in the universe and wishing them respite from their suffering. There is a detailed guided meditation on compassion at the end of this chapter.

sympathetic joy

The third heavenly quality is sympathetic joy. This is the ability to rejoice at the happiness of others. Instead of thinking that happiness is limited and another's share will take away from your own, you see that rejoicing with other people actually adds to your happiness. There is no limit to love or happiness. Rejoicing with others liberates you from small-mindedness and resentment. Rejoicing in your own happiness, you acknowledge and appreciate fully the good things in your life, and you stop comparing yourself with others:

May your happiness not leave you.
May your good fortune not diminish.
May your joy continue.

Again, open your heart to yourself, looking beyond what you like or dislike about yourself, and reaching out to the human being who is breathing and has the potential for happiness. Appreciate your good fortune and the joy you experience in this moment, and wish for it to continue. Then move through the sequence from the people close by to all the living things in your vicinity, to friends, to those you feel neutral towards, to enemies and, finally, to all beings. Rejoicing in their happiness will help you to be more light-hearted and expansive.

sitting on a chair

equanimity

The last heavenly quality is equanimity. This balances the first three, so that you are not overwhelmed by either love or compassion or joy. You experience those feelings but you do not grasp at them, you do not over-react. Like a mirror, you reflect completely what is present and when that is gone you let go. You realize you cannot live other people's lives for them. You want to help, you feel for them but you cannot change them – only they can do that. But you can still love them, feel for them and rejoice with them, with a calm and clear mind, with equanimity. The verse for the meditation on equanimity is:

May I accept things as they are.
May I be open and balanced.
May I find equanimity and peace.

There is a guided meditation on equanimity at the end of the next chapter, 'Non-attachment'.

Loving-kindness is an antidote to ill will and anger; compassion to cruelty and the desire to hurt; sympathetic joy to apathy and indifference; and equanimity to resentment. By meditating you are not trying to become perfect but to create more space and love in your life. Practising the four heavenly abodes is about your intention to meditate and cultivate certain qualities. While you are meditating on each of the four abodes, your mind and heart are benevolent. The concentration and enquiry that are cultivated during this exercise will help you be more present to yourself and your own conditions, as well as to the predicament of other people. When the meditation ends, a sweet taste will remain that will flavour your life with a calm and deeply-felt joy.

guided meditation: compassion

- Find a quiet place and sit in a comfortable posture.

- Settle yourself in this place, at this time. There is nothing else to do but offer empathy and compassion, in this moment, to yourself and others.

- Now open your heart and place your awareness on yourself. Look beyond what you think you are like. Reach out to the human being who can feel pain and suffering, and wish yourself well, steadily repeating this verse:

May I be free from pain.
May I be free from sorrow.
May I be free from danger.

- Now expand your awareness and bring your concern to the people around you. Take each person in turn. Look beyond what you think they are like, and reach out to the human being who is alive and suffers like you. Wish each one well, while repeating the verse several times.

- Now expand your compassion to everything that is alive outside – plants, trees, insects, animals, people. Like you, they too do not want to suffer. Open your heart and wish them well, repeating the verse.

- Now open out your empathy to people you like. Look beyond what you like about them and reach out to the human being who is breathing and can be in pain. Wish them well, repeating the verse.

- Now expand your awareness to the people you feel neutral towards: a shopkeeper, a bus conductor, a neighbour. They too have a history that is very real to them. They too love and suffer. Take each of them in turn and wish them well, repeating the compassionate verse.

- Now bring your compassion to people you have difficulties with. Look beyond what you dislike about them and reach out to the human being who, like yourself, suffers when in pain. Wish them well, inwardly repeating the verse.

- Finally, expand your awareness and open your heart and concern to all beings:

May all beings be free from pain.
May all beings be free from sorrow.
May all beings be free from danger.

non-attachment

We often limit ourselves by sticking to our preconceptions. Non-attachment means caring without grasping. With non-attachment we can flow through life, experiencing each moment fully without trying to hold onto it.

non-attachment

grasping

Non-attachment does not mean that you do not care. Non-attachment means that you do not grasp. We have a tendency to grasp at and then stick to everything we come in contact with, through hearing, tasting, seeing, touching, smelling and thinking. This grasping is at the root of much suffering. Let's imagine that I am holding an object made of gold. It is so precious and it is mine — I feel I must hold onto it. I grasp it, curling my fingers so as not to drop it, so that nobody can take it away from me. What happens after a while? Not only do my hand and arm get cramp but I cannot use my hand for anything else. When you grip something, you create tension and you limit yourself.

Dropping the golden object is not the solution. Non-attachment means learning to relax, to uncurl the fingers and gently open the hand. When my hand is wide open and there is no tension, the precious object can rest lightly on my palm. I can still value the object and take care of it; I can put it down and pick it up; I can use my hand for doing something else. If you do not uncurl the fingers, your holding becomes one with what is being grasped and you are taken over by it. You see the precious object outside its context, you are blinded to other possibilities and reduced to what you are holding. Non-attachment is part and parcel of equanimity and leads to a more spacious approach to life. Non-attachment is not indifference but, on the contrary, leads to true caring and compassion. If a mother hugs her baby too tightly, the baby will feel uncomfortable and cry. But if she holds her baby too loosely, the child is likely to fall. So the mother must hold her baby just so, not too tightly and not too loosely.

People usually cling to things like those burdock burrs that children throw at each other's clothes. Through the senses, you come into contact with something — whether good or bad, difficult or easy — and a certain process of grasping begins. After grasping at the word, the thing, the situation or the relationship, you identify with it, stating that this is 'me', 'mine', 'happening to me'. Then you solidify the experience, saying to yourself that it is real, for all times and all situations. By doing this, you limit yourself. You reduce yourself to what you are grasping — being like this, having that problem, being affected by this painful word or that unpleasant experience. The process makes you magnify an object or a situation until it becomes a monster that totally

overwhelms you. You end up feeling helpless and out of control. But this process does not need to happen. Non-attachment can help you dissolve the patterns of grasping.

limiting yourself

A few years ago, I was travelling in America with Stephen. In California, we were invited to join a well-known meditation teacher for an evening talk. Until then, I had never given a talk to more than forty people, but in that audience there were more than two hundred! When the time came for me to speak, I could not. I was struck dumb, grasping at the fact that I had never spoken to two hundred people before. I had identified myself as somebody who could only talk to forty, which limited me to a number. Two hundred people were magnified into *two hundred, impossible*! I froze. Fortunately, Stephen was there to take over. Afterwards, I reflected on what had happened and was mortified. I felt I had let the side down because at that time people often commented that there were very few women teachers and I had been unable to speak.

There and then I realized that there did not need to be a difference between forty and two hundred. I decided that in the future I would speak, no matter what the circumstances. Some time later, a friend who was organizing a conference for six hundred people unexpectedly rang up to ask if I could replace a speaker who had fallen ill. I replied that I could – no problem. I went, I talked, it was well received. And only afterwards did I tell the friend that I had never spoken to so many people before. His face was a picture – one moment reflecting the worry that it could have been a disaster and the next relief that it had gone so well!

There are so many things you can grasp at. If you understand the concepts of non-self and emptiness, you will realize there is no separate self to grasp. But you might still grasp at a specific part of this flow of conditions that forms your relative self.

your appearance

You might grasp at your body or at a part of your body. You might reduce yourself to being tall or short, fat or thin, and become obsessed with changing yourself. Of course, if you are unhealthily thin or overweight, you might be able to change that by dieting. But be careful not to reduce yourself to one aspect of your body, because you risk magnifying that aspect until it takes over your life.

your traits

You might grasp at a certain characteristic, describing yourself as a 'good' or 'bad' or 'angry' person. If you have a tendency to get angry in certain circumstances, try to understand why, but do not reduce yourself to a single quality. You are not good or bad or angry twenty-four hours a day, day in, day out. Sometimes we think of people as all good or all bad. But 'goodness' and 'badness' depend on mental and emotional tendencies, on inner conditions and outside circumstances.

Gandhi's life was exemplary in many ways and he is a great role model, but he was rather unkind as a father and made his sons very unhappy. Sometimes young people are told that they will never amount to anything. They hear everyone telling them they are bad and then they think they might as well be very bad, since there is no hope for them. They are reduced to one tendency, but making a tendency more than it is will only reinforce it. What can you do instead to weaken the negative tendencies in your own mind and in the minds of young people?

your work

You might grasp at your work or at your role within society. It is natural to identify with your work; it is what gives you self-worth, makes you active and sustains you financially. However, as soon as you grasp at your role, you limit yourself. You might be a teacher and like teaching because it gives you knowledge and power. So you continue to be a teacher outside the classroom – and then wonder why your friends are sometimes reluctant to meet you.

A meditation teacher once stayed at my house for a few days, and from morning to night she did not stop teaching about awareness and awakening. It became quite tiring after a while. Remember that your role is only one among the myriad conditions that form you. You can have so many different roles in your life. One moment I am a teacher, the next a student, a daughter, a wife, a friend, a counsellor. Non-attachment will help you to flow through these different roles, to inhabit each one fully and dance on to the next without grasping at any of them.

your relationships

It is easy to become attached to people and to your relationships with them – to partners, children and friends. Notice what happens when you do. You want to grasp at people because they are nice, because they make you feel happy or safe. So you stick to certain people and try to spend as much time as possible with them. But by doing this you

crowd them and stop yourself from making other connections. When I was first married and had just arrived in England, I used to stick to Stephen like glue. I was always next to him at the dinner table or on the sofa, and followed him around until I realized that this was not healthy either for him or for me. I saw that he was feeling stifled and I was being prevented from making friends with other people.

When you love people, you care for them and want to be with them but you cannot become one with them. You are separate individuals who can influence each other, grow together and support one another. Part of your experience is shared but another part is your own. Two individuals in a relationship are like parallel lines that run close to each other but never conflate; the space between the lines is shared but the space outside is distinct. You can create more space between the lines but you must not forget that there is also space outside. Your outside experience also contributes to the relationship. The more each of you grows as an individual, the more the relationship will grow and develop. No relationship can remain stationary because both individuals will continue to change and grow in response to their mental, emotional and physical conditions and external circumstances.

You also have to be careful not to grasp at the expectations, projections, images and ideals that you have about other people. These images are not real. What is the point in grasping at them? The more you expect of people, the more suffering you will cause them and yourself. Non-attachment does not mean that you do not have hopes and aspirations, but do not grasp at these either. In a relationship, it is essential to get to know, accept and appreciate the whole person, not just

the bits you like. If you have difficulties with somebody, discuss the problem and see if it is the other person who needs to change or your own attitude. I have a friend who was in a serious but chaotic relationship. Whenever I met her, I would ask her how it was going. One day, she told me that she had decided to stop trying to shape her boyfriend to her own ideas and needs. Since she had begun to accept him as he was, she was finding the relationship much easier. Instead of arguing, they could laugh at each other's foibles and enjoyed being with each other much more.

your possessions

You can become attached to material things. Sometimes you accumulate possessions as a way of bolstering the ego. This is dangerous because you limit yourself to these things and if they go, you go too. The more you have, the more you are afraid to lose and the more you become upset when your possessions are damaged. Let's say you buy a new car. You are delighted with it. But watch yourself as some children playing with a stick come by and see if you get anxious and angry. If the car does get accidentally scratched you explode: how can this be happening to your new car! How dare they damage it! But by wanting the car to stay in its pristine new condition, you are grasping at something that by its own nature cannot last.

You need material things such as food, shelter, clothes and medicine. You can use these skilfully, without them owning you, by looking at them with a creative and reflective mind. For example, we can become quite attached to the taste of certain delicacies, like asparagus, and will go to great lengths to get them. However, although asparagus is delicious, if you had it every day it would lose its specialness. After two months of eating asparagus you might even become fed up with it and yearn for something more ordinary.

Money is essential for getting by in the modern world but it is often used as a benchmark for evaluating success and happiness, and it is easy to become obsessed with it. Ajahn Chah, a twentieth-century Thai master, pointed out that if chicken shit were the currency you might not grasp at money so much!

Thai abbots and monks are renunciate and live a simple life. They are supposed to own only eight objects: three sets of robes, one bowl, water, some medicine, a needle and thread. But it seems that for this reason people give them presents. The room of a Thai monk is often full of many different objects like tennis rackets, exquisite vases and golden watches. A young Western monk visited Ajahn Chah once and remarked that he had a beautiful glass on his table. He went on to ask whether this was not against the rules, since Ajahn Chah was a monk and a renunciate. He replied that the glass was indeed beautiful and useful to drink from but when he used it he saw it as already broken. Looking at the glass in this way, he did not grasp at it.

your surroundings

If you become so attached to a place that you never want to leave, you stop yourself from discovering anywhere new. And then if you are forced to move, you might be unable to appreciate your new home because you are always comparing it to somewhere else.

After living in Korea for ten years, I moved to a beautiful part of Devon by a river among the rolling green hills. For the first six years, I thought of my surroundings as not bad but not nearly as nice as Korea. Then, one day, as I was walking in the sunshine along the Devon lanes, I looked and looked again and at last the beauty of my surroundings hit me. I had finally let go of the other place. Korea was beautiful and green; Devon was too, in its own way. Be careful of grasping at places and carrying them in your mind as somewhere good or bad. Grasping because you perceive something as good is the same as rejecting because you perceive it as bad. It is the same process of identification, solidification and magnification.

your opinions

You might grasp strongly at views, opinions, ideas and theories. But what are these? At one level, views and ideas are simply synapses firing in the brain. Whenever you have an argument or a political discussion, notice what happens. You have an idea and immediately you identify with it: this is my idea and therefore it defines who I am; if you do not agree with my idea, you are rejecting me. From 'my idea' you progress to 'a good idea' to 'the right idea' to 'the only idea' – and then you fight to the death to defend it. In a proper dialogue, you behave differently. You appreciate ideas as creative thoughts and, although you prefer some to others, you realize that there are different ways of looking at a situation. Believe in your views without grasping at and identifying with them, and you will be more creative and spacious in your thinking.

Ideas are powerful and they can lead to great achievements. But when they are disengaged from the ordinary realities of daily living, and the consideration that people are different, ideas can also cause great suffering. By grasping blindly at ideas, however beautiful or clever, you can become removed from the present experience and dehumanized.

Someone once asked me for advice about her relationship with a friend. She complained that they would go for walks in the country but spend the whole time arguing about the hot issues of the day. I suggested that she pay more attention to their surroundings: the softness of the grass, the whiteness of the blossoms, the freshness of the air. Then, as they walked together, she should feel the earth beneath her feet and try to listen to her friend without getting entangled in discussion that had very little relevance to their lives. She found that by doing so the friendship deepened and they were more caring and present for each other.

Ideas are tools and do not have intrinsic meaning in themselves. They are conditioned by the circumstances that formed them. You might be sure that you have found exactly the right theory to solve a certain problem, but in most fields such theories are constantly being replaced by new ones that are better adapted to the latest circumstances. Be careful that by grasping at a certain theory you do not limit yourself to it and narrow your potential and possibilities. Theories and ideas can help you to lead a better life if you use them skilfully but do not solidify them. Any one theory cannot explain the complexity of life and define you for all time.

your culture

People are often very attached to their cultural and national habits. This grasping is insidious because as long as you stay in your own country you will not realize what you are doing. Living in Korea for ten years was a great lesson in humility. Until then, I had thought my way was the natural way of doing things. In Korea, I realized that my way was just the French way; very useful when in France but definitely not appropriate in Korea. Whenever Koreans saw me doing even something simple like wringing clothes, they would commiserate because I could not do it properly. And of course they would show me the right way – the Korean way. It was actually quite difficult to change my habits. I was happy to learn but the muscle co-ordination did not seem to be there.

Cultural habits are deeply embedded in our mind, speech and body. They are the first habits we acquire as young children and the last we can let go of. In Korea, a tiny six-year-old once showed me how to wash clothes; she got quite impatient when I did not do it in the proper way. You cannot exist without cultural habits. But can you be yourself, without grasping and identifying with cultural norms, using what you have grown from wisely and skilfully? Can you learn to be more adaptable and flexible? Try to practise non-grasping and non-attachment in your own small way, wherever you are.

your past

You might grasp at past experiences. These are your personal compost; you are made of past experiences but you are not reducible to them. Remember that they have been absorbed and replaced by other experiences, they are finished and gone. Painful experiences can be a shock to the system and it is hard to let them go; you have to realize that you do not need to drag the pain of the past into the present. By focusing on what has happened you reduce yourself to the past and stop yourself from completely opening to what is now. Do not judge the grasping, try to soften it by becoming more present.

We become attached to pleasant experiences and straightaway want to repeat them. Whenever I have had a fun weekend with friends, I say, as they are leaving: 'That was so much fun, let's do it again!' But 'doing it again' is a dream, a mirage — nothing is repeatable. You can have hopes and aspirations but you can never predict how things will turn out.

I love couscous and whenever we go to Paris one of my treats is to eat couscous in a good North African restaurant. The last time we visited Paris, I had not eaten couscous in a long time and the meal was delicious. Three days later we went again to the same restaurant and, though the couscous looked exactly the same, it was not quite as tasty as the first time. Was this because of the quality of the food or because I had grasped at a specific experience, trying to repeat something that could not have the same intensity the second time around? I would

prefer the answer to be the quality of the food because then there is still hope of repeating that delicious experience. But I do not think it is!

your non-grasping

You must also be careful not to grasp at meditation, Buddhism or even the present moment. Meditation is very beneficial but not a panacea. It has its own place and context. Buddhism gives you a worthy way to live but does not have all the answers. The present moment is already gone so you cannot grasp at it, even if you wanted to. But you can flow through the present moment, you can interact with it creatively and inhabit it. The less you grasp, the lighter you will become. You will naturally create space in your experience. Your innate wisdom and compassion will arise more easily as there will be no walls to obstruct them.

In Korea, I used to translate for Western monks and nuns. Once I took an Australian monk to meet an old master, who was highly respected. He lived a very simple life in a small room, without putting on any airs. The first question the monk asked was what he could do to help monks and nuns who were not practising hard. In reply, the master told him a Zen story:

There was a master with two disciples. The first disciple meditated day and night, his back straight and his eyes wide open. The other disciple would fall asleep whenever he sat in meditation, his head lolling on his chest. One day, the master approached the second disciple and said to him:
'Look at the other disciple and take him as an example. His back is straight, his dedication is formidable, he never sleeps.'

Then the master went to the first disciple and said to him:
'Look at the other disciple and take him as an example. He is not attached to meditation or to any forms, he does not identify himself as a meditator. He practises so well that he constantly falls into such a deep concentrative state he is not aware of his body. You should truly follow his example.'

The master we were visiting pointed out that one can never know the state of meditation in another person, and so we should not pass any judgement.

There is a Zen story about what can happen when you grasp at precepts:

Two monks were walking along the bank of a river and they came to a low point where they could cross. On their side of the bank was a woman who was in distress, fearing that the river was too swollen for her to cross. One monk offered his help and carried her over. The woman thanked the monk profusely and they went their separate ways. However, as the monks were approaching their monastery, the second monk began to look more and more upset until he exploded: 'How could you carry that woman? It is against the rules! As monks, we must never touch a woman.'
The other monk replied calmly:
'I left her by the river but you are still carrying her.'

There is another Zen story that illustrates non-grasping and compassion:

A monk was practising in a hermitage near a small village in Japan. One day, the parents of a young woman discovered that she was pregnant. They pressed her to tell them who the father was and she finally burst out that it was the monk. When the baby was born, the grandparents rushed to the small temple and knocked forcefully at the door. The monk answered the knock and they told him:

'This is your child.'

'Ah, so,' the monk replied, taking the baby kindly in his arms. Thereafter he took great care of the child. A few months later, the daughter confessed that the father was actually a young fisherman. So the parents rushed back to the monk and told him they were sorry but that this was not his baby.

'Ah, so,' he said and gently gave back the child.

The monk did not grasp at the child when it came or when it left, but offered his compassion while it was needed. He did not judge the daughter or the family, he neither asked for explanation nor presented any. He just responded to the situation at hand, as it came to him. At times it is good to let non-grasping happen and to respond to a situation just as it is. We have a tendency to think too much and complicate matters. Non-attachment creates the space that allows us to respond simply and directly.

p r a c

patience and tolerance

The tendency to grasp is so strong that you need great patience to dissolve it. Meditation helps you to weaken negative mental and emotional habits but tolerance is also required towards yourself and these habits. Rome was not built in a day; non-attachment takes time. It is necessary to give yourself time and space in the practice of meditation. You must be careful not to grasp at the desire to have everything resolved now.

patience

Master Ajahn Chah said that:

Desire in practice can be a friend or a foe. At first it spurs us to come and practise. We want to change things, to understand, to end suffering. But to be always desiring something that has not yet arisen, to want things to be other than they are, just causes more suffering.

Naturally you want to progress rapidly, but meditation is an organic process involving all of your body and mind and it takes time to learn to concentrate and enquire, to let go and not grasp, to develop a kind and soft mind. You must be patient with yourself and try again and again with renewed enthusiasm.

Do not try to go too fast or take shortcuts. Take one meditation at a time, one experience at a time, one day at a time. You are not trying to achieve something fixed and specific. Just meditate for its own sake, resting in your potential in this moment, nurturing yourself patiently. Be wary of the tendency to want things to happen fast and in a certain way, just so that you can move on to the next thing and then the next. Meditation is a lifelong journey; that is what gives it its beauty. Patience with yourself will allow you to enjoy the journey all the more.

tolerance

A tolerant mind is an open and spacious mind. It is the opposite of a grasping and restrictive mind. When I was in Japan, I met a nun who had been practising all her life. I asked her about her practice and what she felt she had accomplished. She told me that she meditated by chanting. Sometimes she would totally immerse herself in it, neither grasping at anything nor keeping anything back, and then she would feel great peace and awareness. However, she considered her main practice that of being tolerant, open and kind to whoever came to her door. She endeavoured to receive everyone equally and tried to listen to people as they were, not as she wanted them to be. Even if she was tired, even if the person was difficult, she tried to keep to that practice. She told me that when she did this successfully, she felt a great sense of accomplishment. I was very humbled and inspired by her example.

106

t i c e

guided meditation: equanimity

- If you can, sit outside on the grass. Remember to keep your back straight and relaxed. Your intention is to cultivate equanimity and non-grasping.

- In this moment, what are you grasping at? If you are grasping at thoughts or opinions, see their unsubstantiality. Let them go. Rest in a spacious mind where thoughts and opinions are as light as bubbles.

- If you are grasping at a sensation, look deeply within it. It is not fixed and solid. It cannot be grasped.

- If you are grasping at a feeling, notice how fleeting and changeable it is. You cannot reduce yourself to it.

- If you are grasping at a loved one, can you dissolve the stickiness and care deeply but without expectations or attachment?

- If you are rejecting a situation or person, see that you limit yourself by magnifying the importance of the situation or the difficult characteristics of the person.

- See the benefit of a quiet and non-grasping mind and repeat this verse:

  May I accept things as they are.
  May I be open and balanced.
  May I find equanimity and peace.

- Now wish equanimity to a neutral person, then to a loved one, then to someone you dislike, visualizing that person each time and repeating the verse, using 'we' instead of 'I'.

- Finish by wishing equanimity to all beings:

  All beings are the owners of their actions.
  May all beings be open and balanced.
  May all beings find equanimity and peace.

- Now open your eyes to everything that surrounds you. Can you be with it, fully present, caring and engaging deeply, without grasping or rejecting anything?

107

awakening

Awakening cannot be reduced to a single
experience. It is a process of dissolution,
which involves letting go completely of
hatred, greed and delusion. you do not
awaken to something external, but
to your own true nature.

awakening

buddhist awakening

At the root of Buddhist meditation is the moment of the Buddha's enlightenment, or awakening. The root of Buddha is *budh*, which means 'to awaken', 'to understand'. So 'awakening' is perhaps a better word to use to describe this moment than 'enlightenment'.

The word 'enlightenment' also has romantic associations; it makes people think of flicking a switch and being suddenly surrounded by light. You might imagine that enlightenment will bring utter peace and contentment, that it will solve all your problems or transform you into a totally different person. You might see enlightenment as liberation from the pain of this world, and equate it with a kind of extinction. Or you might be attracted to the heroic nature of the word and fantasize that through enlightenment you will save the world.

a state or process?

When you meditate, it is possible to experience various states in which you feel different from your usual self. Are they awakened states? Do they lead to permanent awakening?

Master Kusan used to say that these states are not an experience of awakening but merely a perception of the luminous nature of the mind. You might feel great joy because you have consciously or unconsciously let go of tension. You might feel incredible lightness because you experience yourself as less fixed than when you are attached to a sense of self. You might become, for a moment, very open and compassionate as you let go of grasping. These states are useful in so far as they allow you to experience yourself differently. However, a special meditative state arises out of the conditions in which meditation is practised and as soon as the conditions stop the state usually evaporates. What you are left with is the memory that things are not as they seem to be, to act as compost to your innate wisdom and compassion.

You might have mystical visions when you meditate. These visions are very much dependent on who you are; they might not have much to do with wisdom and compassion. The litmus test is whether these experiences make you wiser and more compassionate or not. The Buddha achieved intense meditative states through concentration exercises but he did not feel that they were the answer to his predicament,

to the questions of life, death and suffering. The Buddha's awakening was not based on achieving a meditative state but on the total dissolution within himself of the three poisons of hatred, greed and delusion. From this experience of awakening the three trainings of ethics, meditation and wisdom were devised.

four stages of ennoblement

In the Theravada tradition, there is a very useful model of awakening called the four stages of ennoblement. In each stage, you become free of certain afflictions that stop you from being fully awakened.

In the first stage, you become free from the erroneous belief in a fixed self and from scepticism about yourself and the practice. You lose your attachment to mere rules and rituals, which you recognize as skilful devices that can be applied or not, according to the circumstances. In the second stage, you reduce the power and influence of greed, hatred and delusion. You greatly weaken the desire to acquire and own things, and also your intense dislike of certain people. Your perceptions and understanding of yourself and the world are less deluded. In the third stage, greed, hatred and delusion disappear. Desire and grasping are replaced by an equanimous mind, hatred by love and compassion, and delusion by wisdom. In the fourth stage, conceit, restlessness and ignorance disappear. This final stage shows that there are always subtler and subtler forms of delusion.

The four stages of ennoblement demonstrate that there is much work to be done and that awakening is not so much about gaining as losing. You do not add something to yourself when you practise meditation, you uncover and develop what is already there and dissolve whatever obstructs that process.

There are four stages in the model so be careful not to get too caught up in the first stage and make the mistake of thinking that that is all there is to awakening. You cannot cling to any one stage of attainment. Every time you lose something, there is still more to lose. You might be free from the notion of personal identity but you still have to let go of conceit. So beware of anyone who says 'I am awakened', since just the fact that they are saying this might prove the contrary. As Nagarjuna, a second-century Indian philosopher-monk, said:

'I am free! I cling no more!
Liberation is mine!'
The greatest clinging
Is to cling like this?

practice and goal

A poem by the nun Mittakali, who was practising at the time of the Buddha, expresses the practice and the goal:

Although I left home for no home
and wandered, full of faith,
I was still greedy
for possessions and praise . . .
Life is short.
Age and sickness gnaw away.
I have no time for carelessness
Before this body breaks.

And as I watched the elements of mind and body
Rise and fall away
I saw them as they really are.
I stood up.
My mind was completely free.
The Buddha's teaching has been done.

You have to be realistic about your expectations of the path and awakening. Otherwise the goal you set yourself might be inappropriate or impossible to realize. This makes me think of a poem by the seventh-century Chinese poet, Hanshan:

Body clothed in a no-cloth robe,
Feet clad in turtle fur boots,
I seize my bow of rabbit horn
And prepare to shoot the devil Ignorance.

how to awaken?

Over time, Buddhists developed different views about how long awakening takes. In the early days, it was thought that it took many lifetimes, many aeons, to become like the Buddha and even then was possible only from a male body – not a very satisfactory view for women! Later, the idea developed that you could become a buddha in your own lifetime if you practised the three trainings of ethics, meditation and wisdom with great mastery and dedication. Finally, it was thought that each person is already a buddha and the only thing to do is awaken to one's own buddha-nature in this moment. This view is expressed in the *Avatamsaka Sutra*, which states:

Sentient beings are buddhas, buddhas are sentient beings.

This statement implies that all beings have the nature of a buddha and can awaken to it at any moment. But buddhas must be humble and remember that they are also sentient beings capable of making errors. One moment you can be a buddha, the next a deluded sentient being. When I was doing some research in Korea, I met a nun who was a student and a follower of the *Avatamsaka Sutra*. She had decided, when she became a nun, to study for a few years to get a good grounding in the Buddhist classics, and then go to meditate in a mountain hermitage in order to become awakened and help as many people as she could. However, as she studied the *Avatamsaka Sutra*, she was struck by the passage about sentient beings also being buddhas and decided to live her life that way. Now she teaches Buddhist texts, among them the *Avatamsaka Sutra*, in a Buddhist university, and her practice is to be a buddha from moment to moment. When she gets up in the morning, her intention for the day is to display and express the wisdom and compassion of a buddha as much as possible. And at the end of the day she reviews how she did because a buddha is also a sentient being and, as a sentient being, capable of making mistakes.

gradual or sudden path?

Today, awakening is viewed differently across the Buddhist traditions. In some schools, awakening is seen as a seed that the three trainings allow you to cultivate and grow over time until it has fully blossomed. This is a gradual, linear view where the notion of purification and progress is very important. You find it mostly in the Theravada tradition and in some Tibetan schools. In other traditions like Zen and Tibetan *dzogchen*, awakening is seen as an actuality that needs

to be uncovered. The practice is then about removing the blinkers that stop you from perceiving your own awakening.

This difference of opinion has led to a great debate about the practice of meditation and its relationship to awakening. In the Zen tradition, the path of meditation is expressed in three ways. There is gradual practice, followed by gradual awakening; sudden practice, followed by sudden awakening; and sudden awakening, followed by gradual practice. Some people within the Zen tradition insist that the sudden practice and sudden awakening path is best, and they dismiss as 'gradualist' anyone who does not follow it.

This debate is false. The gradual and sudden paths to meditation are both essential and are encompassed in the practice. Your practice stands at a crossroads formed by the intersection of the two paths. The gradual path represents width of practice. You put in effort, patience and a long-enduring mind, which over time bear fruit: meditation becomes easier, the mind is calmer and clearer, you become wiser and more compassionate. The sudden path represents depth. Suddenly you have insight, you see clearly the way things are. As you let go of certain mental and emotional habits, you have a glimpse of states of liberation. You do not consciously force yourself to have these insights, they just happen.

The founder of our monastery in Korea, Master Chinul, advocated the third way: sudden awakening followed by gradual practice. He said later that this would in turn be followed by another sudden awakening, to be followed by more gradual practice. Master Chinul pointed out that before you can step confidently and surely onto the path, you need a sudden insight, however small, to show you the way and give you great faith. And because delusions and habits are powerful, you have to cultivate gradual practice patiently in order to actually put your insight into action and embody it in the world in an experiential way.

Two ancient Chinese Zen poems describe the two aspects of practice. The first is by the eighth-century master, Shen-hsiu:

The body is the enlightenment tree
The mind is like a clear mirror
At all times you must wipe it clean
And must not let the dust collect.

The second is by the Chinese Sixth Patriarch, Hui-neng:

Enlightenment originally has no tree
The mirror also has no stand
Buddha-nature is always clean and pure
Where can dust alight?

Your practice needs to be both gradual and sudden. If you only think in terms of gradual development, you can become narrowly deterministic, trying to fit everything into a fixed set of actions and results without allowing for the differences between people. However, if you focus only on the sudden dimension of practice, you can become too mystical and idealistic, and lose touch with reality. And with this approach, ethics are often the first to go. You need to be simultaneously open to both approaches. Practise regularly, without expecting a definite result, and at the same time be open to the awakening that might break through at any moment.

not a geographer

What do you expect awakening to do for you? Have you been told that it will give you perfection and omniscience? Even the Buddha was a man of his culture and time. He inhabited the Indian world of 500 BCE, when the earth was flat and its centre was Mount Sumeru. For this reason, Buddhist cosmology is not scientifically accurate. As the Dalai Lama has said, the Buddha was not a geographer. And even in his own world, he was not able to accomplish everything he set out to do. He tried three times to stop a war between neighbouring states and did not succeed – but that did not stop him from trying.

Even the Buddha had his headaches. His monks and nuns caused a lot of trouble and laypeople regularly complained about their behaviour. At first there were no monastic rules. As time went on, the monks and nuns became more numerous and more mistakes were made. Each time this happened, the Buddha enacted a new monastic rule. By the end of his life, he had created hundreds of rules to regulate the life of the monks and nuns. Awakening is the culmination of cultivating thoroughly the three trainings of ethics, meditation and wisdom, and realizing your full potential. It has little to do with perfection or omniscience.

Master Kusan had three awakenings. In his being, he was spacious, wise and compassionate. He was adaptable to any social circumstance. People would ask him difficult questions and I often worried about whether he would be able to answer them. He always did, creatively. He was also kind, understanding and easily available. Another teacher in Korea might want people to bow to the Buddha three thousand times before he would meet them; anyone could meet Master Kusan at any time. However, he was not perfect or omniscient. Time and time again, I saw that he was embedded in his culture and experiences, and could not understand things that were outside that context.

I travelled abroad with Master Kusan several times. When we returned, he would tell the people of the monastery about the trip. Once, when he was describing his travels on the east coast of America, he said that in Boston he had seen the spot where Christopher Colombus had arrived. Earlier, I had tried to suggest that he had visited the place where the *Mayflower* had landed. But he would not change his mind because Christopher Colombus was what he had seen and understood.

On another occasion in Los Angeles, the temple there borrowed a television to show a Buddhist video. The television remained for a few days afterwards and the monks started to watch ordinary programmes. One day, Master Kusan started wondering why we were so quiet and came down to check on what we were doing. He found us all around the television watching reruns of *The Invisible Man*. He sat with us for a few minutes and then remarked: 'He is there, ah, he is not there.' I tried to explain that the programme was about an invisible man but Master Kusan could not understand what I meant. He had not been raised with television and had no frame of reference for this 'invisible man' that was so obvious to the rest of us. On another occasion in Paris, Master Kusan asked me about the Seine and would not believe me when I told him that it is the fourth largest river in France. He was convinced that it is a purpose-built canal and not a river, because it has concrete banks. So Master Kusan was a great teacher but no more of a geographer than the Buddha.

a process of ungrasping

When you use the word 'awakening', what do you think it means? Are you referring to a certain experience or a permanent state? Awakening cannot be reduced to a single experience and replicated as such. It seems to me that awakening is a process of ungrasping, of letting go, of shedding. It is not a permanent state that is transcendent and outside the conditions that we inhabit. I have met many great teachers and they have all impressed and inspired me with their wisdom and compassion, but again and again I have been surprised that they are unable to go beyond their own culture and experiences. This showed me something about my own expectations of what I would call the popular idea of awakening. Now I believe that you awaken to your own nature, not to something outside of it. You awaken to what is there, to what you cannot see very clearly at this moment. Master Kusan used to say that sometimes it feels like you are separated from awakening by a wafer-thin piece of white paper, very light but still obstructive. Huang-po, a ninth-century Chinese master, said:

When at last in a single flash you attain full realization, you will only be realizing the buddha-nature that has been with you all the time.

Awakening, enlightenment, might not be what you think or hope it is. Shibayama Roshi, a twentieth-century Japanese master, used to say that what you think of as awakening does not actually exist but is a dream, a mirage. Looking for awakening is sometimes compared to a fish looking for water: it awakens when it realizes that it is already swimming in it. Many Zen stories are about this moment of awakening:

Chao-chou asked Nan-ch'uan: 'What is the Way?'
'Ordinary mind is the Way,' Nan-ch'uan replied.
'Shall I try to seek after it?' Chao-chou asked.
'If you try for it, you will become separated from it,'
responded Nan-ch'uan.
'How can I know the Way unless I try for it?'
persisted Chao-chou.
Nan-ch'uan said: 'The Way is not a matter of knowing or
not-knowing. Knowing is delusion, not-knowing is confusion.
When you have really reached the true Way beyond doubt,
you will find it as vast and as boundless as outer space.
How can it be talked about on the level of right and wrong?'
With these words, Chao-chou came to a sudden realization.

In the Zen tradition, there is a series of paintings called the 'Ten Oxherding Pictures'. You can often see them on temple walls. These images of the search for and capture of a lost ox illustrate the stages of practice on the meditative path. The last four images describe the different facets of awakening. The seventh image, 'Forgetting the Ox, the Oxherder Rests Alone', shows the oxherder quietly sitting at home gazing at the moon. At this stage, there is no separation between mind and body, spiritual and non-spiritual: everything is meditation. The eighth picture, called 'The Ox and the Oxherder are both Forgotten', in which neither the ox nor the oxherder appear, represents the stage of realization where there is no separate 'I'. You no longer think 'I' am meditating; meditation just happens. Nothing is 'me' or 'mine'; you experience yourself as a flow of conditions and things are not solid or fixed any more.

However, awakening does not stop there. The ninth image is called 'Returning to the Original Place'. This is the stage of realization that you are not separate from the world but are intimately connected with it. Everything that surrounds you can teach you about awakening: a bird song, blossoms swaying in the breeze, your car stopping at a red light. You experience interdependence and connection with all of life, and you act from that knowledge. The last image, 'Appearing in the Market Place with Gifts', shows that the practice is not just for yourself but for the sake of all beings. Awakening is not passive but active and creative. You respond to the world with compassion and wisdom. You lead a simple life, adapting to different social circumstances, and try to bring joy and peace to those you meet, giving what is needed and appropriate.

This sequence of images describing awakening does not necessarily represent a linear, unbroken pattern. Like a spiral, the series might be leading up or down. Even when you are going up, you will reach a stage that you have encountered before, but it will have a different focus or intensity and will ask you to go beyond the known, beyond what you are used to.

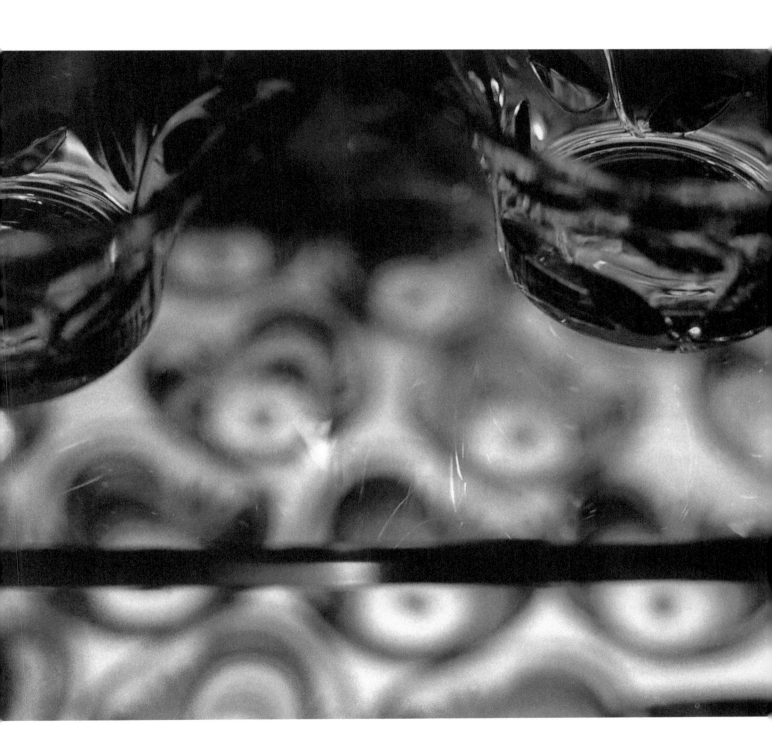

p r a c

zen questioning

Zen questioning is a simple and direct method that helps you uncover your own buddha-nature. It was developed in China from the sixth century onwards, in reaction to the scholastic tradition of the time, which relied heavily on the scriptures. The Zen school wanted to get back to the Buddha's original message of practising meditation and realizing awakening in this life. Zen questioning uses *koans* – past stories of awakening – as a starting point for meditative enquiry. There are seventeen hundred official Zen *koans* and new ones are created all the time.

what is this?

'What is this?' is the question used most often in Korean Zen practice. The first time it was recorded was when Hui-neng, the Chinese Sixth Patriarch, was visited by a young monk:

The young monk, Huai-jang, had walked many days to reach the patriarch. When he met him, the patriarch asked: 'Where do you come from?'
'From Mount Sung,' replied Huai-jang.
The patriarch asked further: 'What is this and how did it get here?'
Huai-jang remained speechless. He could not answer and remained to practise and ponder this question. After eight years he had an insight and went to the master.

'What is this?' asked Hui-neng.
'To say it is like something is not to the point. But still it can be cultivated,' replied Huai-jang.

The whole story is the *koan* but its essential point is the question 'What is this?' The practice is very simple. Whether you are walking, standing, sitting or lying down, ask repeatedly 'What is this?' You are not looking for an intellectual answer so your question should not be an intellectual enquiry. In this moment, you are turning the spotlight onto yourself and your whole experience. You are not asking: 'What is this thought?' or 'What is this sensation?' If you need to put the question into a meaningful context, you are asking 'What is it that is thinking?' or 'Before you think, what is this?' You are not asking 'What is the taste of the tea,' but 'What is it that tastes the tea?' or 'What is it before you even taste the tea?'

Master Kusan used to point out that what you question is not an object because it cannot be described in terms of size or colour. It is not empty space because empty space cannot ask a question. It is not a buddha because it is not yet awakened to buddha-nature. It is not the master of the body, the source of consciousness or any other designation, because these are mere words and not the actual experience of what it is. So you are left with the questioning. You ask 'What is this?' because you do not know.

Concentration and enquiry are combined in one method in this technique. Concentration is developed as you come back again and again to the words of the question. 'What is this?' is the fixed point of the meditation; it brings you back again and again to the present moment. The question is alive but you are calm and focused when you ask it. In that moment of experience, you are aware of everything as you ask the question diligently and sincerely.

Enquiry is vivid because the words are not repeated like a mantra. In themselves, the words do not have special resonance nor are they sacred. They function as a diving board to help you throw yourself into a pool of questioning. Do not put special emphasis on any specific word of the question. The most important part of the question 'What is this?' is the question mark.

Question unconditionally without expecting anything. Give yourself totally to the question. Zen questioning is like diving, which engages the whole body as you jump, not just the arms or legs. Then the whole body and mind are refreshed as you dive into the cool pool. Try to develop a sensation of questioning similar to the bewilderment you feel when you have lost something. You are going somewhere and you put your hand in your pocket to grab your car keys. They are not there. Before you try to rationalize and think of where else they might be, there is a moment when

you are totally perplexed. This is very similar to the sensation you are trying to develop in Zen questioning.

Questioning makes you more open and flexible and creates space in your mind. It gives you energy because there is no place to mentally rest or grasp. It allows for less certainty, more possibilities and the kind of wonderment with which a young child discovers and marvels at the world. It means being immediate and responding in a creative way to the situation at hand, and not being lost in the future or the past. It is not trying to explain away or judge or analyse. It is just being with the moment, looking deeply, asking 'What is this?' and being open to experience as it is.

the questioning method

There are different ways to meditate with Zen questioning. The easiest is to ask the question in combination with the breath. Breathe in and then, as you breathe out, ask 'What is this?' Master Kusan used to suggest asking the question as a circle. Start with 'What is this?' and as soon as one question is ended start another 'What is this?'

An alternative is just to ask the question once and remain for a while with the sensation of questioning.

121

As soon as it fades away, bring back the feeling with another question and again stay with the pregnant sense of questioning till it dissipates. You have to be very careful not to ask the question in an intensely intellectual way. Ask from the belly or even from the toes. You need to bring energy down the body and not focus it in the head. If the question makes you feel speculative, confused or agitated, just come back to the breath, to a simple and calming practice.

the full lotus position

You are not trying to force yourself to find an answer. You are giving yourself wholeheartedly to the questioning. The answer is in the questioning itself, in the tasting of the question. When you tell children who have never seen snow that it is white and cold, they might think of a piece of white paper in the fridge. If you show them the top of a mountain in the distance, they might imagine that snow tastes like coconut ice-cream. Only when they touch the snow, play with it and taste it do they really know what snow is. And with the question 'What is this?' the tasting is in the questioning itself.

Master Kusan had three awakenings and yet he still continued to ask the question. A Western monk asked him why this was because surely, after three awakenings, he must have found the answer. Master Kusan told him that the questioning does not work that way. As you meditate, the practice develops in its own way and slowly evolves. So, of course, we asked him how he practised the questioning now. He would not answer; he said that we had to find out by ourselves because any description of his would lead to misconceptions on our part.

The most important thing in Zen questioning is for the question to remain alive, for your whole body and mind to become a question. In Zen they say that you have to ask with the pores of your skin and the marrow of your bones. As a Zen saying points out:

Great questioning, great awakening; little questioning, little awakening; no questioning, no awakening.

guided meditation: 'what is this?'

- You are sitting in a quiet and secluded place. Your back is straight. You are poised, at ease and attentive. Your eyes are half-closed, gently gazing in front of you.

- With the first few breaths, connect the question to the outbreath. As you breathe out, ask 'What is this?'

- As you continue, the questioning becomes a circle. As one question ends, steadily start the next 'What is this?'

- You are not repeating the question like a mantra, you are developing a sensation of perplexity, asking unconditionally 'What is this?'

- This is not an intellectual enquiry. You are not trying to solve the question with speculation or logic.

- Do not keep the question in the head, try to ask it from your belly.

- With the whole of your being, ask 'What is this?' 'What is this?'

- The answer is not found in a thing, or in empty space, or in the Buddha, or in a designation.

- You are asking 'What is this?' because you do not know.

- If you become distracted, come back to the question again and again. Let the question be like a stick to which a goat is tethered. As the stick stops the goat from eating the crops, so the question keeps you centred, away from passing thoughts, feelings and sounds.

- The question 'What is this?' is an antidote to distracted thoughts. It is as sharp as a sword. Nothing can remain on the point of its blade.

- By asking this question deeply you are opening yourself to the whole of your experience, feeling deep wonderment and awe.

- When the session is finished, move your shoulders, back and legs, and gently get up with a fresh and quiet awareness.

the role of a teacher

The task of a teacher is to empower you,
to wake you up to your own inner teacher.
The true teacher works to make himself or
herself redundant. And life itself is the
supreme teacher, presenting you
with challenges at every turn.

the role of a teacher

is a teacher essential?

I was told in Korea that to practise meditation well you need three things: a good environment, a good community and a good teacher. A good environment is a place that is propitious to meditation and encourages awareness. A good community is a group of like-minded people who share your interests and concerns and will help, support and challenge you along the way. A good teacher is someone who has integrity, is a good guide and can show you the way not just through the teachings but through his or her actions.

In books about meditation, meeting a teacher is often singled out as the most important part of the spiritual quest. I have met many people who are looking for a special teacher, the one destined to help them reach awakening. However, finding that teacher is more easily said than done. I have a friend who looked for many years until she found the one teacher with whom she could feel the moving mystical experiences she wanted. I was pleased for her, as she seemed so happy, though I wondered to myself how long it would last. When I met her three years later, the initial high had faded, she had left her teacher and was back to square one. But I met her again recently and she seemed at peace. She told me that she had

finally found her own inner teacher and that this was what now inspired her on the path. Ultimately, the aim of meditation practice is for you to uncover your own potential, to become your own teacher. A teacher is there to empower and not to disempower you.

During the free seasons in Korea, when I was not on retreat, I used to seek out the great teachers. I regularly visited Master Kyongbong, who lived high up in a mountain hermitage about an hour's walk from Tongdosa monastery. Once, I entered his room, bowed three times as was the custom and asked him to give me advice on how to keep the Zen question bright and vivid. Master Kyongbong acknowledged my presence but did not reply. When I pressed him by asking the same question again, he just said: 'You know already.' As he refused to say anything else, I finally left and walked back, feeling a little resentful about having come all that way without getting an answer. Then suddenly I understood. I realized that Master Kyongbong did not have to tell me about any special methods because I did indeed already know what to do. By challenging my assumption that he knew best, he had caused my inner teacher to wake up.

the guru

In Buddhism, there are three different ways of being a teacher. In the Tibetan tradition, the teacher is seen as a lama, or guru. He is considered to perform the function of the Buddha himself. Any progress that you make on the path is linked to the kindness and blessing of your teacher. It is thought that without such a spiritual teacher, who has gained wisdom from his own teacher, who in turn has received instruction down a lineage of ancient masters, it is impossible to have any living access to the wisdom of the Buddhist tradition. The lama is often considered more significant to the student's actual practice than the historical Buddha. In the Tibetan tradition, this is called guru yoga practice. It involves taking special vows in which you promise not to think badly of or criticize your teacher. You must have total faith as you surrender yourself to your teacher's higher wisdom.

A teacher like this can provide help and inspiration beyond his or her immediate presence because of the great faith of the follower. A Tibetan Buddhist nun from England, who was living as a hermit in the Himalayas, was once trapped in her cave by a freak blizzard. It was pitch black inside and when she finally managed to open the door of her cave, she found a wall of ice. Trapped in this small space, the nun thought she was going to die. She felt calm, thinking that the only thing that really mattered was her lama. She prayed to him from the depths of her heart and at that moment heard a voice inside her that said: 'Tunnel out!' She eventually did just that.

Surrendering is a powerful practice but also a perilous one, if the teacher is not very accomplished. For this reason, you are advised to spend many years checking out potential teachers before becoming a disciple. You have to find out if your chosen teacher is wise and compassionate and would be good for you. The model of the teacher as guru suits people who benefit from devotional practices.

the master

The second model is of the teacher as a master or *roshi*. This style of teaching is found in the Japanese Zen tradition. It is inspired by samurai training and is a challenging discipline in which you have to prove yourself. The *roshi* tests you constantly, trying to trick you in order to help you move beyond attachment and develop patience and endurance. You build a very intimate relationship with your teacher, who is supposed to know you better than you do yourself. In this relationship, loyalty is vital and leaving one teacher for another mid-training is discouraged. The method can be effective if you need, and like, a certain amount of discipline.

As the respected Western Zen master, Kapleau Roshi, explains in *The Three Pillars of Zen*:

The roshi is alternately the strict and reproving father who prods and chastens and the gentle loving mother who comforts and encourages. When the student slackens his effort he is coaxed or goaded, when he displays pride he is rebuked; and conversely, when he is assailed by doubt and driven to despair he is encouraged and uplifted. An accomplished roshi thus combines stern detachment with warm concern, flexibility and an egolessness that can never be mistaken for weakness or flabbiness, in addition to self-confidence and a commanding air.

the friend

The third model is that of the good friend or *kalyanamitra*. You find this model of teaching in Korea and in the Theravada tradition of Southeast Asia.

The *kalyanamitra* is seen as an ordinary person, who has been practising for some time and so knows more than you do. This sort of teacher acts a guide on the meditative path, there to give you instruction and encouragement, and to act as example and inspiration.

When I was first in Korea, I often used to visit Master Kusan to ask him questions about Zen. After a while I stopped, because I realized that the most important thing was to put his instructions into practice. However, he was essential as an embodiment of awakening, as a living example of what was possible on the meditative path. His presence – his lightness, wisdom and compassion – were inspiration in themselves. When he died it was like a light had gone out, as if a huge spiritual vacuum had been created in the monastery. Although we respected and appreciated him when he was alive, it was not until after his death that we were struck by how indispensable Master Kusan's intangible presence had been.

With the third model, you can consult several teachers, so long as you are not confused by too many conflicting instructions.

What was heart-warming in Korea was that teachers would send you to other teachers as a matter of course. There was no hint of competition among them. I myself was told several times by one teacher to go and visit another because the first felt the second to be more knowledgeable or experienced. Personally, I prefer the third method because it seems to lead earlier to a certain autonomy and is less likely to give rise to dependency. This third method also seems more practical. Although there are many teachers to choose from, there are few with whom you could develop a close relationship, as most are quite popular and busy, travelling from place to place around the world.

Your choice of teacher is also affected by where you are and who you have access to. You can always start from books but books might not necessarily be able to answer your specific questions or help with personal difficulties. You need to look around, see if you know anyone who has done some meditation or check if there is a centre with respected teachers in your area.

the four reliances

When you are looking for a teacher it can be useful to take into account the four reliances of the Tibetan tradition.

The first reliance is to 'rely on the teaching and not on the person'. This means that you have to be careful about being attracted to a teacher solely because he or she is beautiful, charismatic or exotically dressed. Don't put your teacher on a pedestal, but rely on what is being taught. Does it conform to the tradition? Is it interesting? Is it beneficial?

The second reliance is that it is better to 'rely on the meaning than on the words alone'. Words can be poetic, inspirational and very seductive. The teacher might be a skilful speaker. But does he or she make sense? What do the words actually mean? You might like to hear the words 'freedom', 'love' and 'enlightenment', but do they really mean something strung together in the context in which you have heard them? Can you apply the instructions contained in these words? Do they still mean something to you when you are no longer in the same room as the teacher who said them?

The third reliance is that it is essential to 'rely on what is unambiguous and not on what is ambiguous'. Spirituality can often be presented in a vague or opaque way. Is this because the teacher does not really know what he or she is talking about or finds it hard to explain in words? The teachings have to be clear and straightforward for you to understand them. Teachers needs to find creative ways to explain clearly what they mean and what they have experienced. Be wary of the way things are sometimes camouflaged and fudged.

Because Zen is challenging and idiosyncratic, I used to think that any Zen teaching was valid, even if it made no sense. Because the teaching was Zen, logic did not matter – until a friend pointed out that even Zen has logic and that any Zen teaching has to make a certain sense.

This realization certainly improved my translations. I was once translating a talk by Master Kusan for a group of Western monks and nuns and used the words: 'Like an eye falling onto a stove, it would melt instantly'. I thought that this was a strange image, and a little bit ghoulish, but told myself that

Zen was weird anyway. Fortunately, I then remembered what my friend had said about Zen having a certain consistency. When I stopped to think for a minute, I remembered that in vernacular Korean eye and snowflake have the same pronunciation. When I realized that Master Kusan must have meant 'snowflake', I changed the translation to: 'Like a snowflake falling on a stove, it would melt instantly' – to the obvious relief of everyone in the room. Zen is strange but not to the extent of creating images worthy of a horror movie.

The fourth reliance is that it is beneficial to 'rely on experiential wisdom and not on knowledge'. Are teachers talking about what they themselves know intimately or just quoting from a text? It is easy to memorize texts by heart and then talk as if you had practised and experienced them yourself. People love to speculate. They become mesmerized by words, principles and theories, and forget that the words have to be put into practice before they can speak from experience. It is easy to talk about freedom, emptiness and awakening but difficult to actually let go, renounce and be non-grasping. Sometimes you have to look beyond what people say and pay attention to how they are and live. Do your teachers practise the three trainings of ethics, meditation and wisdom, or only one of them, or none at all? If they follow only one of the trainings, they might be very proficient in that area but they will not be able to teach you about every aspect of the practice.

expectations and projections

You have to be very careful about how you view teachers. If you put your teacher on too high a pedestal, you will make your own goal so much further away. And you can tie yourself in knots by imagining that your teacher is omniscient. While I was in Korea, a French monk came to study with us. He was convinced that since Master Kusan was supposed to be awakened he must be able to read minds. So whenever he went to see Master Kusan he would try to make his mind blank. He became very nervous before every interview, even though he had requested them himself. I kept trying to tell him that, to my knowledge, Master Kusan could not read minds, but he would not believe me.

Misconceptions like these often occur because of what you hope the practice will do for you. Sometimes students actively want to study under someone who displays supernatural powers. This would then be proof of the teacher's greatness, some of whose glory might reflect onto them. In the Zen tradition there is an injunction:

When the master raises his eyebrows or blinks his eyes, do not think that he is giving instruction about the meaning of the Zen question.

You have to be cautious about what you project onto teachers who you believe to be great and exalted. When you project in this way you disempower yourself. You elevate another person at the price of putting yourself down. On one occasion while I was travelling with Master Kusan in America, we went to visit a certain Buddhist centre. The young man who showed us around was very excited about being able to spend time with Master Kusan. Suddenly he asked me: 'What did Master Kusan mean by that profound and mystical gesture? Please ask him.' I was a little perplexed by the question but turned to Master

Kusan and asked anyway. He replied that he had been brushing away a fly!

the inner teacher

One of my favourite stories is about a monk who lived alone in a hermitage:

Every day the monk called out to himself: 'Master!'
and answered: 'Yes, sir!'
Then he would say: 'Be wide awake!'
and answer: 'Yes, sir!'
He would add:
'Henceforward, never be deceived by others!'
'No, I won't!' he would reply.

You need a guide but you also need to awaken to your own teacher. You cultivate your inner teacher by having confidence and trust in yourself and in your own wisdom and insight. Master Kusan had three awakenings. When he presented his teacher with his understanding his teacher told him: 'Until now you have been following me; now it is I who should follow you.' Teachers are not there to keep you subordinate. On the contrary, their role is to make you grow and surpass yourself and them.

transmission from the past

In some schools of Buddhist meditation, especially in the Tibetan and Zen traditions, transmission is seen as vital. Each of these schools can trace its lineage back to a great master or to the Buddha himself. In the Tibetan tradition, the power of a teacher resides not only in personal achievement and understanding, but in the fact that each is the reincarnation of a great lama. In the case of Zen, the power of teachers lies also in the formal recognition of awakening (the 'Dharma Seal'), given to them by their own teachers, who in turn received it from their teachers, and so on. This also confers on them permission to teach. However, some teachers appear out of nowhere without any apparent line of transmission. Can they not also be considered the heirs of the Buddha, so long as they have vanquished what all the great teachers vanquish: greed, hatred and delusion? True transmission is keeping the spirit of the Buddha alive though the practice and by responding compassionately and wisely to whatever presents itself to you.

In ancient times, different traditions and cultures rarely came into contact with each other's wisdom. Nowadays, teachers from the different Asian schools of Buddhism can easily meet each other at Buddhist conferences and international religious gatherings. It might be natural to assume that these teachers would agree with each other, especially as they are all supposed to know about the same thing – awakening. However, this is rarely so. The teachers are all embedded in their own culture and personal experiences, and often have little time for other practices and traditions. For example, Master Kusan was convinced that the Korean Zen method was superior to any other and often told me so.

Western Buddhist disciples in Asia often like their master to engage with masters of other traditions. It usually ends in disappointment. One day, a group of Zen students wanted their Korean master to talk to a great Tibetan lama who was teaching in the vicinity. A meeting was organized and the students had great hopes for it, expecting something momentous to happen between these two awakened people. The two masters met and straightaway the Zen master decided to be very Zen. So he grabbed an orange, showed it to the lama and asked: 'What is this?' The Tibetan lama turned to his interpreter and asked him: 'Don't they have oranges in Korea?'

Slowly the situation is improving as teachers travel more and encounter different cultures and traditions. As the ancient

Asian traditions meet in the pluralistic West, dialogue is possible and becoming very constructive.

the ethics of teaching

Be careful not to give too much adoration and power to teachers. You will be very disappointed if you discover they have feet of clay. You might find they are causing suffering by seducing vulnerable young women or men. They might be amassing money for themselves. They might be blinded by power, their sole aim to increase the number of their followers regardless of circumstances. There are many ways in which unethical teachers will justify themselves. The best excuse I ever heard was given to a nun who was visiting Thailand. There she was approached by a monk, who told her that the best way to gain awakening would be to have sex with him. Needless to say, she refused the offer and moved on!

A teacher might be greatly accomplished in meditation but still disregard ethics. And that is the *raison d'être* for the three trainings of meditation, ethics and wisdom. Some teachers claim to be beyond ordinary ethics. Other teachers might depreciate wisdom and tell you that it is not necessary to think. Some might be ethical but very narrow-minded and somewhat unkind. Others might be dogmatic and claim that only they know the pure teaching and that everybody else is wrong or impure. You need to use your wisdom and discrimination when seeking and following a teacher.

Sometimes the best teachers are those who do not see themselves as teachers. In Korean monasteries, the meditators encourage each other by telling stories of hard practice. I kept hearing about a monk who for years had worked all day and meditated all night. I wanted to meet him to get some pointers and I finally tracked him down in a small temple. When he saw me, the monk did not know what to do. He could not understand why I wanted to receive teachings from him. He told me that he was an ordinary monk, not a master, and he had nothing to say. Finally he relented and gave me some instruction about the practice but very reluctantly and only because I had come such a long way and was an honoured guest.

You can learn by listening to teachers and you can learn through their example. Good role models will demonstrate the benefits of the practice by the way they live. You can also learn by not following in the footsteps of a bad role model. Teachers have to inspire confidence in their training and experience but they also need to cultivate humility and know that there is always something more to learn. You will be able to teach someone something and, in turn, someone else will be able to help you. Life itself is the supreme teacher, offering wonderful opportunities but also challenging and confronting you at every turn.

p r a c

obstacles to meditation

Meditation is a wonderful tool but it is not always easy. There are some obstacles that are commonly encountered when you begin to meditate.

pain

The most immediate of these is pain. Even if you sit comfortably in a chair, your body will not be used to sitting still and you will feel pain in your back or shoulders. If you sit on the floor in one of the cross-legged positions, your feet might go to sleep and give you pins and needles. You might get cramp in your knees or ankles. If you kneel, you will use different muscles in your knees and ankles, and these might hurt too.

The first thing to ascertain before you begin to meditate is whether you have a medical condition affecting your knees, ankles or back that could be exacerbated by your posture. If you do, meditate sitting on a chair. If you cannot sit on a chair, you will have to meditate lying down, walking or standing, and you may have to keep the periods of meditation short.

If you do not have any physical problems, choose a posture that fits your body; some people are more supple than others. When I started out, I had bad knees because of a skiing accident but I discovered that the sitting posture actually improved them. To my surprise,

within a month of sitting for ten hours a day, I was able to sit in the full lotus posture. When you are young, your body will usually adapt to the various postures and become more supple. However, you should not push yourself too hard. If the pain persists after you have finished a sitting meditation session, change your posture or sit in a chair. If the pain disappears as soon as you relax your legs, it was only due to the position and the length of time you were meditating.

When you begin to practise, you will not be used to meditating so your mind will be tight and the whole process might feel uncomfortable. Over time, your mind and body will become used to the discipline and it will be much easier. You will relax into the posture and the meditation. Then you might notice that pain depends on your state of mind.

If you are lost in day-dreams, time will pass swiftly and you will not notice any pain. If your mind is properly concentrated, you will not grasp or magnify the sensations you experience. However, one is usually half-distracted and half-concentrated, and this half-and-half state will make you notice painful sensations more. If this happens, it is useful to enquire, to go into the sensation you experience in your knee or ankle, instead of reacting to it and fixing it in the mind. You will find that the sensation of pain becomes fluid, that it pulsates and changes.

136

t i c e

People are different. Some of my friends can sit cross-legged in meditation for up to two or three hours, without any problem. I am not like that. After thirty minutes, I start to feel pain and generally I do not sit for more than an hour at a time. If you sit once a day for thirty minutes, you should not experience too much pain. If you sit several times a day, your leg muscles might be protesting by the end. Remember that there are also three other postures – walking, standing and lying down – and try to experiment with all four.

sleepiness

Another obstacle you might encounter is sleepiness. I have a friend who falls asleep as soon as he begins to sit, which makes it very difficult for him. He spends a lot of time devising ways to keep himself awake. The first thing to do is to check your back. You need to sit up straight in order to keep awake; as soon as you slouch, your mind will become cloudy. As you sit in meditation, check your posture from time to time and straighten the back if necessary. The second remedy for sleepiness is to open the eyes wide, without focusing on anything or looking about. Just gaze very gently in front of you. The third remedy is to reflect on death, on the preciousness of the moment. Bring into your consciousness the fact that you could die tomorrow; this will make you more awake in the moment. The fourth remedy for

the standing position

137

sleepiness is to take a short, brisk walk before meditating in the sitting or lying-down posture.

Look at the conditions that give rise to sleepiness. You could be physically or mentally exhausted. You might need to lie down and rest first, and meditate later. If you feel sleepy while you are sitting but as soon as you stop meditating feel wide awake, perhaps sleep is your habitual means of escape from being in the moment. If you sit after lunch or dinner you will probably feel drowsy, as all your energy is going into digesting your meal. There are times during the day when you feel brighter; try to sit then to help your meditation be fresh and clear.

restlessness

Restlessness is the opposite of sleepiness and can be an obstacle as well. When you first meditate, you might feel uncomfortable, itching here and there as if you were sitting on an ant hill. If you do not feel settled, the only remedy is to sit totally still, without moving at all for a while. Your mind might also be agitated and busy. Remember you intention to be awake, to be aware, to meditate and to apply yourself again and again.

expectations

Your expectations can be a major obstacle to meditation. Sometimes you can have too great an expectation of yourself and the meditation. The greater your expectations, the more difficult it will be to attain exactly what you are expecting. This will create frustration and you might be disheartened. Do not be too hard on yourself.

Sometimes the practice will go well, sometimes it will not. This should not stop you from doing it. Intention, direction and inspiration are essential and will give energy to the meditation. Expectations act as a block.

thoughts

Do not try to make your mind blank and without thoughts. The natural activity of the mind is to produce thoughts. When you meditate, you are not intending to stop this mental activity. You are just trying to make the process lighter and more spacious by not grasping and not following the thoughts. They come and they go; just let them be. If you become lost in your thoughts, remember your intention and come back to the focus of concentration again and again. Sometimes you might feel bombarded by internal images or sounds. You might hear a pop song playing in your head, for example. Do not react, do not try to stop it, do not become mesmerized by it. If you just let your thoughts come and go, and do not stick to them or magnify them, they will soon disappear of their own accord.

guided meditation: conversation

- You are having a conversation with a friend. Try to listen with awareness and attention.

- Listen to what your friend is actually saying, not to what you want them to say.

- Be spacious; do not prepare what you are going to say.

- Do not wait impatiently for an opening to say something you consider more important or interesting.

- Try to stay present and not to stray into the past or the future.

- Be attentive; do not make mental shopping lists as your friend is speaking.

- Listen with patience and openness. Try not to react too strongly to the words and events that are being recounted.

- When you respond, let your innate wisdom and compassion do the talking.

- Notice the language you are using. Is it open-ended or does it fix and judge?

- Express yourself directly but with kindness and without speaking harshly.

- Are your words helping the other person to understand you and to make the situation better?

- Rejoice in your own goodness as well as in your friend's, as you share this moment.

- Talking together, can you reach a greater understanding and contribute to a genuine dialogue?

- As you finish the conversation, can there, for a few seconds, be space for silence and a different kind of communication; an awareness of being alive in this moment together?

daily life

You do not need to confine yourself to meditating in the four positions. Awareness, concentration and enquiry can be practised anywhere — you can meditate as you work, communicate, rest, travel and love. Bring a meditative attitude to everything you do!

daily life

formal meditation

You can make both formal and informal meditation part of your daily life. Formal meditation means taking the time to meditate in silence in one of the four postures. It is useful to do some formal meditation every day in order to become familiar with meditation and to develop a consistent practice.

The easiest way to meditate formally on a regular basis is to do it when you lie down in bed at night and when you wake up in the morning. As you lie in bed, watch the breath for a few minutes before falling asleep. If you wake up during the night, instead of worrying about not sleeping or thinking about your problems, try to meditate, relaxing the body and breathing softly and attentively. When you wake up in the morning, watch the breath for a few minutes, becoming aware of bodily sensations or listening to sounds without grasping at any specific sensation or rejecting any particular sound.

In the morning, you could meditate in the sitting posture for ten minutes or more, using a quiet place you have set up for the purpose or just a chair at the dinner table, if you are on your own. It is not quantity you are looking for but quality time to meditate without interruption. Ten minutes of concentration are preferable to thirty minutes if meditating for the whole half-hour would make you feel rushed. On the other hand, if you are too busy to find any time at all you might want to question your timetable. For some people, afternoons or evenings can be a better time to meditate. The hour is not important, what is essential is finding the time to stop.

In the modern world, we often feel like we are on a treadmill, constantly occupied and doing, not only physically but also mentally and emotionally. Formal meditation is useful because it allows us some breathing space. You need to balance all this doing with just being, with resting in awareness. Sitting, walking, standing and lying down in formal meditation will remind you of what you consider beneficial and essential in your life. Formal meditation is a remedy for being trapped in the activity and the doing. Though it is easy to identify with your work, you should not limit your sense of self-worth and identity to working. You need to work, to be active, to express yourself and be creative, but this activity has to be balanced by periods of quiet reflection, of stillness and silence. It is rare to be able to find and cultivate silence nowadays because

our time and surroundings are full of activity, people and background noise. Rest in meditation daily by focusing on simple objects such as the breath, sensations or sounds.

Think of daily formal meditation as similar to brushing your teeth or eating three meals. You do not question the usefulness and necessity of these everyday activities. Meditation is food for the spirit. It is not an exotic activity that can only be practised on mountain tops in the East. You can meditate anywhere – in your living room, your kitchen, your bedroom. You might choose to create a small meditation corner, with a cushion, chair or stool. You could add an inspiring picture or quotation, or flowers or some other natural object that is pleasing and calming. This meditative corner will remind you of your intention to meditate and the values you cherish in your life.

If you are inspired to practise formal meditation for a longer period, you can meditate for a weekend, a week, a month or more on group retreats in various meditation centres, Buddhist or otherwise. If you would rather practise on your own, you could go on holiday to the countryside. If you plan to do a longer meditation retreat, it is advisable to develop a firm basis for your practice by starting with a group retreat led by a teacher, since the support of other participants and the wise guidance of a teacher can be very helpful. When you become more familiar with the practice, it will be easier to sit on your own.

However, be wary of romantic ideas about hermits and caves in the Himalayas. Very few people are able to meditate in solitude for long periods of time. I have a friend who was a hermit in the Himalayas for ten years. Whenever she went to visit her teacher for a few days, she would offer her cave to other meditators. They found that even with the best intentions in the world none of them could live that life for more than two or three days.

informal meditation

You do not have to be in one of the four postures to meditate. During the day, there are 'nothing happening' times that can be used to watch the breath informally. Instead of being bored or irritated when you are stuck in a traffic jam, realize that you have been given a good opportunity to meditate. Before you distract yourself from the 'nothing happening' moment by reading a magazine, making a phone call, watching television or having a cup of tea, just meditate for a few minutes, quietly watching the breath.

You might get angry and impatient when you are waiting for a bus but these feelings of irritation will not make the bus come any faster. However, if you use the time to cultivate concentration and enquiry, when the bus does come you will feel light and calm instead of sour and agitated. And you will be kinder to the bus driver!

Meditation can be a tool to prevent stress. When you start to think that you are too busy, you feel under pressure and become tense. Notice when you are becoming anxious, stop a few minutes and just sit still in silence. Come back to your breathing, to the fact that you are alive in this moment. Paying attention to simple physical sensations of contact, such as your buttocks touching the seat of the chair or your hands resting on each other, can be very helpful. After a few minutes, resume your activity and if, later, anxiety and the feeling of busyness again arises and your mind begins to grasp, stop and refocus on the breath or on basic sensations. In this way, you will remain centred and calm, and will not get lost in mental stories and your reactions to busyness.

A school in Somerset had a new toilet unit built, which included one hot-air hand-dryer. For a while, all the teachers admired the cleanliness and efficacy of the new dryer. Then, because they were busy and always in a hurry, they started to complain that using this dryer took up too much time. The teachers asked the school administration for something faster and a rolling hand towel was installed. However, one teacher continued to use the dryer. She was a meditator and found the time spent drying her hands a useful opportunity to meditate, to come back to being centred and calm. Drying her hands meditatively was an opportunity to dissipate the stress brought on by the busy atmosphere of the school.

Informal meditation can be practised anywhere, at any time, simply by using awareness, concentration and enquiry in your daily life. You notice what is really happening to you and other people and you approach the situation creatively, breaking out of your mental and emotional habits. For meditation to work it cannot be confined to the formal postures. The postures help us to develop the discipline of meditation, of a focused and enquiring mind. For awareness to transform the way you are and behave, it has to be activated in daily life. You meditate as you relate, work, rest, travel and love. You can bring a meditative attitude to anything you do.

at work

Master Kusan was always the first to go to work, be that preparing Korean ravioli for a hundred people or tilling the fields. The monks used to hint that they would rather exercise by playing football, but Master Kusan urged them to chop wood or dig instead. Whenever I visited Venerable Songkyong, a respected Korean nun and a great meditator, I would find her gathering acorns to make jelly, or sweeping leaves. This was not glamorous work, it did not make her feel important and special, but it was steady and focused. Venerable Songkyong suggested that such work was a good way to sharpen the practice of enquiry. As I was sweeping the leaves mindfully, I was encouraged to bring a deep sense of questioning to the moment itself by asking: 'What is it that sweeps the leaves?'

In the Zen tradition, physical work is seen as essential and integral to spiritual work. Often the teacher judges one's degree of attainment according to the way one works. It is easy to be inattentive, and as soon as you stop being mindful something goes wrong. Working meditatively is about 'doing' sincerely and efficiently, without attachment or grasping either at the self that is acting, the activity or the result. Working meditatively also connects you to others and to the place where you work. Enquiry helps you to reflect on how you work and the way you relate to your colleagues and your working environment. Respect and care for other people and your environment are prerequisites to a meditative working relationship.

in daily life

On a silent retreat, you practise in defined and disciplined circumstances that allow great depth of meditation. In daily

145

life, you practise within a wide range of uncontrolled conditions as you interact with a world that constantly throws surprising situations at you. Meditation helps you respond creatively instead of reacting negatively. Formal meditation helps you develop an awareness that can be activated as you meet circumstances in your daily life. Part of informal practice is to remind yourself of your values and intentions. Remember and cultivate your intention to be aware and awake. Be determined to develop wisdom and compassion. The influence of the modern world, which encourages you to spend and compete, and your own mental, emotional and physical habits will counteract your values and intention to practice.

Practising only on retreats, in controlled circumstances, will not be enough to effect change and transformation. You need to apply creative awareness throughout your life. The creative awareness you display depends on you and your particular circumstances; no two people are the same. You have to find your own way to meditate in daily life and bring your own creativity to the process. There is no blueprint. Not everyone is a meditator in Korean monasteries. At the beginning of their career, there is a training period when monks and nuns study and meditate together in large groups. After that they choose their own paths. Some become full-time meditators and perhaps go to hermitages in the mountains. Some become accountants, others farmers, painters, scholars, doctors, abbots and abbesses. They do some formal meditation early and late in the day but most of their practice is done informally, as they go about their tasks.

One nun I met started out in the usual way by studying and planning to meditate as soon as she finished her studies.

However, half-way through her studies she fell ill, became interested in the healing process and started to study Eastern medical techniques like acupuncture and herbal medicine. Now she is a doctor, which is very rare for a Korean nun. I asked her how she deals with men, since Buddhist precepts state that a nun is not supposed to touch a man. She told me that she treats both sexes equally and sees each patient simply as a human being that is suffering.

Another nun I met was a singer and a disc-jockey for a Buddhist classical music radio programme. She was also in charge of another radio programme called *Helping Our Neighbour in Difficulty* and worked some nights on a Buddhist telephone helpline too. I was surprised that she was a singer and involved with music, as one of the precepts for nuns forbids singing or listening to music. But for this nun music was connected to her religious feelings and to questions about how we should live and love one another. She saw herself as a lamp that in a small way, through music, illuminated these feelings and questions. For her, music was a creative means of conveying how to love and have compassion for other people.

learning from life

By responding compassionately and meditatively to situations, you learn from life itself. When I was researching meditation in Korea, I finally managed to interview a nun who was very busy and difficult to pin down. A famous scholar and lecturer, she belonged to the Korean council of elder nuns. She also visited prisoners in jail. She had initially only been asked to give one talk but she began to visit regularly as her views of the prisoners changed. She realized that many were in prison because they had acted out of desperation, and she started to see them as ordinary people rather than as 'criminals'. From then on she tried to befriend the prisoners and to help them let go of their bitterness. She encouraged them to reflect on the causes and effects of their actions and she pointed out that since their thoughts and actions came from a seed within themselves, they would have to look at themselves carefully if they wanted to live more contented lives.

I asked the nun how she managed to find time to meditate, when she was obviously so busy. She replied that she meditated while she was being driven around. People would often send a car and a chauffeur to collect her, so she would just sit back and meditate asking the question 'What is this?' in between engagements.

Meditation cannot prevent difficult things happening to you, but a meditative attitude can help you deal with them. Pang Kwihi, a Buddhist lecturer and successful novelist and scriptwriter, is physically disabled and cannot walk. In her youth she had hoped to study to become a doctor but at that time no medical universities in Korea would accept a disabled student. Her only choice was a Buddhist university. She started the study of Buddhism without faith but as she studied she became attracted to its practices and philosophy. For Pang Kwihi, meditation is not just about sitting still. She endeavours to be mindful throughout the day, trying not to speak thoughtlessly. By leaving home with that intention, she finds that even if she has to spend time with someone who is hard to get on with, she can maintain her peace of mind and not hurt the other person or herself.

modern meditation

Sometimes meditation is seen as separate from the material world and inaccessible from modern life. Yet all that is necessary to bring a meditative attitude to this busy modern life is a questioning and creative mind. Then anything you come across, however materialistic, can be turned into a tool of meditation.

working

In Taiwan, I met a nun who had been recommended to me as a great meditator. She was light and very calm and I assumed that she must meditate all day long. In fact, she was the accountant of a huge monastery. I asked her how she could reconcile money and meditation. She replied that she had no problem at all because at the end of the day, as she counted each note that had been given to the temple, she would recite the name of Amitabha, the Buddha of Infinite Light. Counting money and meditative practice were one.

Venerable Manhwa, who was in charge of the English Department in the same monastery, encouraged her students to cultivate inner peace. When her own inner peace was disturbed, she would recite the name of Kuan-yin, the Bodhisattva of Compassion. She used every opportunity to recite this name, to remind herself to keep her heart open to compassion. So instead of grumbling when she climbed up or down the seven-storey staircase in her department building, she would take the chance to recite the name of Kuan-yin.

A friend of mine was a Zen monk for many years until he decided to go back into the world. He moved to New York, where he finally chose to work for a public relations firm, whose clients were commercial as well as non-profit-making companies. When he started work, he put a sign that read 'Meditation Hall' above his front door, where he would see it every morning as he left for the office. The sign was to remind him that the whole of New York could be his meditation hall.

He once had a difficult client and just talking on the phone to this person would make his blood boil. As soon as he had put the phone down, his practice would be to deliberately intensify the angry feelings in order to know them fully. Then he would tell himself: 'That's it, just stop and dissolve this.' And the hot feelings would dissolve because he had made a conscious practice of seeing through them. Instead of being blinded by his angry feelings, he let himself experience them totally in order to realize that all they did was hurt him.

listening

Meditation practice is not just about inner work but also about your actions in the world. It is part of informal practice to be of service and respond with compassion to other people. This can be as simple as practising compassionate and aware listening. As I tried to show in the guided meditation on conversation at the end of the last chapter, you need to ask yourself what form your communication takes. How can you listen and talk with wisdom and compassion? Each conversation can become a meditation in itself if you bring open awareness to it by listening without preparing what you are going to say, by not impatiently waiting for the other person to stop talking, by not over-reacting to what they say and by not listening with just one ear. Listening is one of the best methods of meditating in daily life because you have so many opportunities to do it.

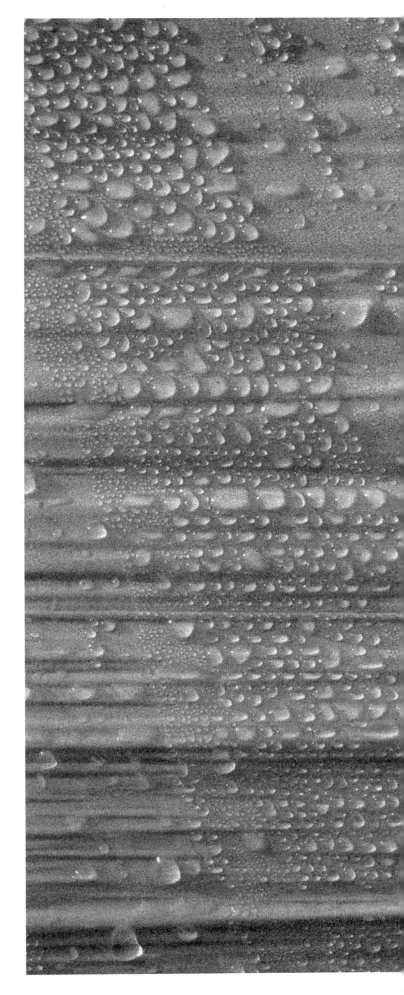

speaking

When you speak you can meditate by trying to be aware of what you are saying and the way you are saying it, your intonation and choice of words. As a foreigner in England, I am aware that I sometimes use a clumsy expression and am grateful when somebody points out that it might be better to say something in a different way. Once, I was told by a retreatant that it did not seem appropriate to use the word 'argue' when I was giving a talk. She felt that saying 'I would argue that' was too competitive and polemical. I took her point and this helped me to be more mindful of my language. Whenever I see that I am about to use the word 'argue', I try to find another word. Generally, I say 'suggest' instead, but am always open to other creative suggestions!

helping

You can become disheartened by the immense extent of suffering in the world. They are so many people suffering from war, famine, illness and poverty. Be wise and realize that you cannot be everywhere at once, that there is only so much that one person can do, and do not let the immensity of the world's suffering stop you from acting and responding as you can.

Venerable Kru is an elderly Thai monk who started out life as a very mischievous young man who caused his parents much trouble. He had a great love of women and his parents lost many cattle as they were often fined for his behaviour towards the girls of the village. In desperation they pleaded with him to become a monk, hoping that Buddhist training would straighten him out. The other villagers hated him. Nobody believed he would stay ordained for very long.

Over time, Venerable Kru changed into a respected monk and finally he went back to his village. When he saw how poor the villagers had become he wanted to help them. Under his leadership, the villagers dug a pond to provide water during the dry season. He also started a rice bank and a buffalo bank to help those villagers who had nothing. He insisted that the villagers work hard together because he saw that this was the only way they would solve their problems. He felt that the village had to be reformed both materially and spiritually in order to survive. The villagers had to be united and work out their own development because they could not rely on anybody else.

Venerable Kru's most remarkable achievement was to build a water pump and construct a truck out of second-hand parts so that the villagers could take their produce to the district market without being indebted to the loan sharks for a means of transport. Some people were scandalized that he was constructing trucks and motorcycles in a Buddhist temple — not something that Buddhist monks generally do! Their opinion did not stop Venerable Kru because his main concern was to help his congregation and do what was needed and appropriate by following his intuition in a creative way. All of you can do this too, in your own way. Ask yourself what your strengths are and how you could be of benefit to others.

the buddhist community

To help develop strength and steadiness in the practice of meditation in daily life, it is useful to meet up with other people who have similar concerns. Your community could be just a few people who meet in each other's living rooms once a month to practise together, and discuss matters related to meditation like mindfulness, reflection, ethics, compassion and the wisdom to know what to do in difficult situations. There are many existing groups affiliated with different Buddhist centres and traditions but there are also groups that are open to anyone. If you cannot start a Buddhist group or find one near you, you can sometimes find groups from other religions or traditions with whom you can share silent times. The Quakers, for example, sit silently together at least once a week and also place great importance on service and helping each other.

The Buddha put much emphasis on community. He saw living in a community as a great opportunity to learn and an important aid in the practice. We need to feel that we are not alone and that others are walking the same path. If you are having a difficult time on retreat, great support can be drawn from the silent presence of others. It is very helpful in daily life if you have some good friends with whom you can share meditation and mutual inspiration. You might want to point out interesting readings to each other, discuss intricate issues or even create ceremonies to bring the group together in a different way.

In America, the Buddhist Peace Fellowship, a long-standing Buddhist organization, created the Buddhist Alliance for Social Engagement programme (known as 'BASE') in 1995. For a period of six months, BASE participants meditate together in groups of around ten, during weekly or twice-weekly meetings and longer retreat periods. At the heart of BASE is a commitment to engage with suffering directly through Buddhist practice.

The participants examine how to bring Buddhist teachings and meditation practices into daily life, and they work and volunteer in organizations such as hospices, prisons, soup kitchens and environmental groups. BASE is rooted in a community of shared purpose; at the end of the six months many participants comment on how much they have learned from the communal part of the programme. The participants seem to benefit equally from the programme's three elements of service, meditation and community.

Along with the Buddha and his teachings, community is seen as one of the three jewels of the Buddhist path. As we meditate, it is important to remember that community is an essential component of spiritual life. In this modern, technologically-advanced world, we are becoming more individualistic and often physically isolated. By developing a sense of community and service, by opening to others and sharing with them, we will enrich our own lives.

prac

dealing with disturbing thoughts

In the Buddha's *Discourse on the Forms of Thought*, he discusses five ways of dealing with the disturbing thoughts that arise either during formal meditation or as you go about your daily life:

think positive

The first method he suggests is:

If some unskilled thoughts associated with desire, aversion or confusion arise and disturb the mind, you should attend instead to another characteristic which is associated with what is skilled . . . It is like a skilled carpenter who can knock out a large peg with a small peg.

The Buddha is saying here that to dissipate a negative thought you have only to think of something positive. As a carpenter removes a large peg with a small one, you could dissolve a heavy, negative thought with a small compassionate idea.

If you are thinking about someone who has hurt you, instead of aggravating the thought by telling yourself that they always do bad things, try to remember the occasions when they have been kind. If you suddenly have an irresistible desire to buy something very expensive that you cannot really afford, instead try buying a small present for somebody and replace

greed by generosity. If you are waiting for someone who is late, instead of immediately thinking that this person has no respect or love for you, question whether there is some good reason for the delay. I was once kept waiting for someone and decided that instead of feeling put upon I would phone to find out what had happened. When I did, I discovered that my friend thought that we had agreed to meet a week later!

know what hurts

The second method of dealing with disturbing thoughts is:

Scrutinize the peril of these unskilled thoughts by thinking: 'these are unskilled thoughts, these are thoughts that have errors, indeed these are thoughts that are of painful results . . . It is like a woman or a man, young and fond of adornment, who if the carcass of a snake or a dog were hanging around their neck would be revolted and disgusted and throw it away immediately as soon as they noticed it.

Here the Buddha is telling us to think about the consequences of our thoughts and to realize that certain types of thought will cause pain. You might think that you are telling it like it is, that you are right and everyone else is wrong. Repeating this to yourself, you become more and more self-righteous until by the time you meet whoever is concerned you are very angry. But as soon as you attack someone verbally, they will get defensive, even if you are in the right. You hurt yourself by getting worked up in this way and you also hurt others.

This method is about letting go of certain thoughts because you see their painful outcome. The Buddha's example is rather macabre but he is trying to make us realize the difficult nature of certain thoughts. When we are lost in our thoughts we see only that they are justified. With awareness and attention, we are able to see the negative effects of these thoughts.

distract yourself

The third method is:

Bring about forgetfulness and lack of attention to those thoughts . . . It is like a man who, not wanting to see the material shapes that come within his range of vision, would close his eyes or look another way.

This method seems to go against the general message of the Buddha, who tells us to be aware and mindful. However, the Buddha is pragmatic and knows the mind well. Some thoughts are too strong to overcome directly and the best way to dissipate them is to change your focus (although in order to do this you first have to see that you are having these thoughts).

If you are fabricating negative unrealities, distract yourself in a healthy way by going for a walk, talking to a friend, reading an absorbing or inspiring book. Do something that will help your mind to change its focus and in that way dissipate the energy and power of negative thoughts.

I used to have a tendency to fabricate negative storylines. One sentence or image would be enough to send me into a spiral of negative thoughts. When I realized this I put into use the second and the third methods of the discourse. First I had to see that the thoughts, however compelling, would lead to painful results. Then, in order not to fall into them, I would distract myself, by reading a novel, for example. The end result was that these kinds of thoughts very quickly stopped troubling me.

This made me realize that if you do not feed the flames of negativity the fire will die out by itself. These methods not only help you deal with the situation at hand, they also, over time, help to diminish and sometimes completely dissolve the arising of certain disturbing patterns of thought.

question your thinking

The fourth method of dealing with disturbing thoughts is to:

Attend to the thought function and form of these thoughts . . . even as it might occur to a man who is walking quickly: 'Now, why do I walk quickly? Suppose I were to walk slowly?' It might occur to him as he was walking slowly: 'Now, why do I walk slowly? . . . Suppose I were to lie down? . . . This man, having abandoned the hardest posture, might take to the easiest posture.

This method brings space and possibilities to your thinking. It helps you look into the root of a thought, it encourages you to question the form of the thought. Why are you thinking what you are thinking? Could you think about something else? Do not ask psychoanalytically but experientially: 'What happened a few minutes ago to lead me to think this?' The Buddha encourages you to then question and be creative with alternative trains of thoughts that could make your life a lot easier.

push it away!

The fifth method recommended by the Buddha is:

By the mind subdue, restrain and dominate the mind . . . It is like a strong man who, having taken hold of a weaker man by the head or the shoulders, might subdue, restrain and dominate him.

This might seem antithetical to accepted psychology that you should not repress anything. Personally, I like the pragmatism of the Buddha. If everything else fails

and you continue to have disturbing and dangerous thoughts, then stop them by pure will power. This is not the only method, it is one among five to be applied when necessary.

The example the Buddha chooses illustrates that your mind is stronger than you think. We tend to believe that our thoughts are stronger than we are ourselves, but that is not so. You cannot reduce yourself to just one thought; you are bigger than this and have more potential. One way to apply this method gently is to say to yourself: 'Let it go for now.'

When a friend of mine has difficulty with his thoughts he says to himself: 'So what! So what!' Someone recently told me that at similar moments she tells herself: 'I hear what you are saying, let it be now.' Both find their tricks work well for them. Each of you can also find creative ways to deal with your own disturbing thoughts. First be aware and have the intention to do something, then creative solutions will arise naturally.

Our minds have so much scope and potential. Why should we let ourselves be burdened by our thoughts? Let's keep in mind one of the Buddha's verses:

The thought manifests as the word;
The word manifests as a deed;
The deed develops into habit
And habit hardens into character.
So watch the thought and its ways with care
And let it spring from love
Born out of concern for all beings.

guided meditation: cooking

- Cooking can be both an art and a meditation. Before you start, prepare yourself.

- If you only have thirty minutes, cook something simple and be creative with the ingredients you have.

- If you have two or three hours and want to cook an elaborate dinner, check that you have all the ingredients you need before you begin.

- Do not be too ambitious. You can produce something delicious with ordinary but well-chosen and well-cooked ingredients.

- Engage with what you are cooking. Notice the characteristics of the ingredients. They will taste different according to how they are chopped and cooked.

- If you want to release the sweetness of certain vegetables like onions or leeks, throw them in a hot pan with a dash of oil. Then the heat should be turned very low and they should be cooked gently for at least five to ten minutes.

- You have to be patient. Cooking certain ingredients takes time. For brown rice, you need a good fifty minutes from start to finish. For basmati rice, thirty minutes is needed, and polenta takes about ten minutes.

- What is more important, to eat or to cook? Thinking about the circumstances and your ingredients will help you to cook with more peace and ease.

- When you cook, be present to the cooking, to the shapes, the tastes, the smells. If you are washing carrots, notice their texture and the feel of the water.

- Keep your expectations realistic. Do not try too hard to impress yourself or others. Cooking is a labour of transformation. What will happen, will happen.

- Try not to identify or grasp at the act of cooking or at what is being cooked. Enjoy, create and explore.

- The busier you are, the slower you should go.

- Remember you are cooking to feed yourself and others, to help yourself and others fully develop their potential.

- Looking into a grain of rice or a handful of flour, see where it comes from – the earth, the sun, the rain, the labour of farmers.

- As you sit on a chair and eat, stop and be present to that moment.

photographer's note

Taking photographs and practising meditation might seem at first glance to be unrelated activities. For while photography looks outwards at the visual world through the medium of a camera, meditation focuses inwards on unmediated experience. And whereas photography is concerned with producing images of reality, meditation is about seeing reality as it is. Yet in taking photographs and practising meditation over the past three decades, I have found the two activities converging to the point where I no longer think of them as different.

As practices, both meditation and photography demand commitment, discipline and technical skill. Possession of these qualities does not, however, guarantee that meditation will lead to great wisdom any more than photography will culminate in great art. To go beyond mere technique in either domain requires a capacity to see the world in a new way. Such seeing originates in a penetrating and insatiable curiosity about things. It entails recovering an innocent, childlike wonder at life while suspending the adult's conviction that the world is simply the way it appears.

The pursuit of meditation and photography leads away from fascination with the extraordinary and back to a rediscovery of the ordinary. Just as I once hoped for mystical transcendence through meditation, so I assumed exotic places and unusual objects to be the ideal subjects for photography. Instead I have found that meditative awareness is a heightened understanding and feeling for the concrete, sensuous events of daily existence. Likewise, the practice of photography has taught me just to pay closer attention to what I see around me every day. Some of the most satisfying pictures I have taken have been of things in the immediate vicinity of where I live and work.

Both photography and meditation require an ability to focus steadily on what is happening in order to see more clearly. To see in this way involves shifting to a frame of mind in which the habitual view of a familiar and self-evident world is replaced by a keen sense of the unprecedented and unrepeatable configuration of each moment. Whether you are paying mindful attention to the breath as you sit in meditation or whether you are composing an image in a viewfinder, you find yourself hovering before a reality that is fleeting and tantalizing.

At this point, the tasks of the meditator and the photographer appear to diverge. While the meditator cultivates uninterrupted, non-judgemental awareness of the moment, the photographer captures the moment by releasing the shutter. But in practice the aesthetic decision to freeze an image on film crystallizes rather than interrupts the contemplative act of observation. Aligning your body and senses in those final seconds before taking a picture momentarily heightens the intensity and immediacy of the image. You are afforded a glimpse into the heart of the moment that meditative awareness alone might fail to provide.

To be moved to take photographs, like being inspired to practise meditation, is to embark on a path. In both cases you follow an intuitive hunch rather than a carefully considered decision. Something about 'photography' or 'meditation' draws you irresistibly. While you may initially justify your interest in these pursuits with clear and compelling reasons, the further you proceed along either path, the less you need to explain yourself. The very act of taking a photograph or sitting in meditation is sufficient justification in itself. The notion of an end result to be attained at some point in the future is replaced by an understanding of how the goal of photography or meditation is right here, waiting to be realized in each moment.

Both meditation and photography are concerned with light. Meditators speak of 'enlightenment': an experience in which light metaphorically dispels the darkness of the mind. Similarly, by means of an odd angle, an unusual arrangement of light and shade or an adjustment in the depth of field, a photographer illuminates something about an object that was previously unnoticed. Such photography has nothing to do with preserving a pictorial record of familiar things, places and people. Instead, it opens up the world in a startling and unexpected way that can be both compelling and unsettling.

The photographer's concern with light is also a real one. For without sufficient light, you simply cannot take a photograph. Yet the closer you attend to what is seen in the viewfinder, the more you notice how the light that illuminates and the object being illuminated are not two separate things. An object is just as much the medium through which light becomes apparent as light is the medium through which an object becomes apparent. You cannot have one without the other. In taking a photograph of an object, you are taking a photograph of a condition of light.

When this separation between what illuminates and what is illuminated begins to dissolve, it becomes increasingly difficult to regard the object being photographed as a thing existing in its own right 'out there'. As soon as you make the perceptual shift to seeing the object as a condition of light, what you observe becomes as tentative, shimmering and luminous as light itself. In paying more attention to the display of light rather than 'something' illuminated by light, photography starts to move away from representation towards abstraction. The photographer becomes absorbed by the restless contrasts of line, colour, shading, what is in and out of focus, to the point where the recognizable object disappears. Likewise, as the meditator deepens and refines awareness, the familiar world of solid things and people begins to dissolve into a play of conditions mysteriously emerging and vanishing.

This is where the path of photography has led me at the time of writing. The images in this book, taken over many years, reflect various stages in the journey. They also mirror my engagement with the process of Buddhist meditation. For both paths have served to deepen my understanding of the fleeting, poignant and utterly contingent nature of things.

Stephen Batchelor

captions to the photographs

further reading

Allione, Tsultrim, *Women of Wisdom*, Ithaca, New York: Snow Lion, 2000

Batchelor, Martine, *Principles of Zen*, London: Thorsons, 1999

Batchelor, Martine, *Walking on Lotus Flowers: Buddhist Women Living, Loving and Meditating*, London: Thorsons, 1996

Batchelor, Stephen, *The Awakening of the West: The Encounter of Buddhism and Western Culture*, Berkeley: Parallax Press, 1995

Batchelor, Stephen, *Buddhism Without Beliefs*, New York: Riverhead, 1996

Batchelor, Stephen, *Verses from the Center*, New York: Riverhead Books, 2000

Blofeld, John (tr), *The Zen Teachings of Huang Po*, Boston: Shambhala, 1994

Buswell, Robert E. Jr (tr), *Tracing back the Radiance*, Honolulu: University of Hawaii Press, 1991

Byrom, Thomas, *Dhammapada: The Sayings of the Buddha*, Boston: Shambhala, 1993

Chadwick, David, *Crooked Cucumber: The Life and Zen Teachings of Shunryu Suzuki*, London: Harper Collins, 1999; New York: Bantam Doubleday Dell, 2000

Chah, Ajahn, *A Taste of Freedom: Selected Dhamma Talks*, Seattle: Vipassana Research Publications, 1988

Chodron, Thubten, *Open Heart, Clear Mind*, Ithaca, New York: Snow Lion, 1990

Cleary, Thomas, *The Flower Ornament Scripture (The Avatamsaka Sutra)*, Boston: Shambhala, 1984

Dalai Lama, *Ethics for the New Millennium*, New York: Riverhead Books, 1999

Goldstein, Joseph, *Insight Meditation: The Practice of Freedom*, Boston: Shambhala, 1994

Gyatso, Tenzin (Dalai Lama) and Geshe, Jinpa (tr and ed), *The World of Tibetan Buddhism: An Overview of Its Philosophy and Practice*, Boston: Wisdom Publications, 1995

Kapleau, Roshi Philip, *The Three Pillars of Zen*, New York: Anchor Books, 1989

Kazuaki, Tanahashi (ed), *Moon in a Dewdrop: Writings of Zen Master Dogen*, Berkeley: North Point Press; Dorset: Element Books, 1988

Kornfield, Jack with Fronsdal, Gil (ed), *Teachings of the Buddha*, Boston: Shambhala, 1993

Leighton, Taigen Daniel (tr) with Yi Wu, *Cultivating the Empty Field: the Silent Illumination of Zen Master Hongzhi*, Berkeley: North Point Press, 1991

Mackenzie, Vicki, *Cave in the Snow: Tenzin Palmo's Quest for Enlightenment*, London: Bloomsbury, 1998

Morreale, Don (ed), *The Complete Guide to Buddhist America*, Boston: Shambhala, 1998

Murcott, Susan, *The First Buddhist Women: Translations and Commentary on the Therigatha*, Berkeley: Parallax Press, 1991

Nanamoli, Bhikkhu (ed and tr), *The Life of the Buddha, as It appears in the Pali Canon*, Sri Lanka: Buddhist Publication Society, 1978; Seattle: Vipassana Research Publications, 1992

Nanamoli, Bhikkhu (tr) and Bodhi, Bhikkhu (ed), *The Middle Length Discourses of the Buddha: A New Translation of the Majjhima Nikaya (Teachings of the Buddha)*, Boston: Wisdom Publications, 1995

Nyoshul, Khenpo, *Natural Great Perfection: Dzogchen Teachings and Vajra Songs*, Ithaca, New York: Snow Lion, 1995

Phongphit, Dr Seri, *Religion in a Changing Society: Buddhism, Reform and the Roles of Monks in Community Development in Thailand*, Hong Kong: Arena Press, 1988

Queen, Christopher S. and King, Sallie B. (ed), *Engaged Buddhism: Buddhist Liberation Movements in Asia*, Albany: State University of New York Press, 1996

Rabten, Geshe and Dargyey, Geshe, *Advice from a Spiritual Friend*, Boston: Wisdom Publications, 1986

Reps, Paul, *Zen Flesh, Zen Bones*, London: Penguin, 1971; Boston: Tuttle, 1998

Ronce, Philippe, *Guides des Centres Bouddhistes en France*, Paris: Noesis, 1998

Salzberg, Sharon, *Loving-Kindness: The Revolutionary Art of Happiness*, Boston: Shambhala, 1997

Sengstan, *Hsin Hsin Ming: Verses on the Faith Mind*, Richard B. Clarke (tr), New York: 1976

Shantideva, *Bodhicaryavatara*, Crosby, Kate and Skilton, Andrew (tr), Oxford: Oxford University Press, 1998

Wallace, Alan (tr and ed), *The Life and Teachings of Geshe Rabten*, Boston and Sydney: George Allen and Unwin Ltd, 1980

Watson, Burton (tr), *Cold Mountains: Hundred Poems by Han-Shan*, New York: Columbia University Press, 1970

Yampolski, Philip B, *The Platform Sutra of the Sixth Patriarch*, New York: Columbia University Press, 1967

meditation centres

There are many different types of meditation centre all over the world. In this brief listing, I have concentrated on centres with affiliated groups in the same country or internationally.

Australia
Blue Mountains Insight Meditation Centre
25 Rutland Road, Medlow Bath, NSW 2780
Tel/Fax: 02 4788 1024
Tradition: Theravada

Bo Moon Sa Temple
317 Canterbury Road, Campsie, NSW 2194
Tel: 02 9718 0315
Tradition: Zen

Bodhinyana Monastery
Lot 1 Kingsbury Drive, Serpentine, WA 6125
Tel: 08 9525 2420
Tradition: Theravada

Hospice of Mother Tara
Buddhist Meditation and Healing Centre
Unit 3, 2B Victoria Street, Bunbury, WA 6230
Tel: 08 9791 9798
Tradition: Tibetan

Open Way Zen Centre
PO Box 993, Byron Bay, NSW 2481
Tel/Fax: 02 6680 8782
Tradition: Zen

Origin Centre (Study and Retreat Centre)
Jeyes Road, Balingup, WA 6253
Tel: 08 9764 1109 or 9764 1275
Tradition: Tibetan

Sydney Zen Centre
251 Young Street, Annandale, NSW 2038
Tel: 02 9660 2993
Tradition: Zen

Tara Institute
3 Mavis Avenue
Brighton East, Victoria 3187
Tel: 03 9596 8900
Tradition: Tibetan

Vajrayana Institute
22 Linthorpe Street, Newtown, NSW 2042
Tel: 02 9550 2066
Tradition: Tibetan

Wat Buddha Dhamma Retreat Centre
Ten Mile Hollow, Wisemans Ferry, NSW 2775
Tel: 02 4323 3193
Tradition: Theravada

Canada
Foundation Vipassana
C.P. 32083 Les Atriums,
Montreal, QC H2L 4Y5
Tel: 514 481 3504
Tradition: Theravada

Gampo Abbey
Pleasant Bay, Cape Breton, Nova Scotia B0E 2P0
Tel: 902 224 2752
Tradition: Tibetan

Sakya Tsechen Thubten Ling
9471 Beckwith, Richmond, BC V6X 1V8
Tel: 604 275 1915
Tradition: Tibetan

Thubten Choling
5810 Wilson Ave, Duncan, BC V9L 1K4
Tel: 604 746 8110
Tradition: Tibetan

Toronto Insight Meditation Center
54 Millwood Road, Toronto, ON M4S 1J7
Tel: 416 932 0327
Tradition: Theravada

Westend Buddhist Center
1569 Cormack Crescent, Mississauga,
ON L5E 2P8
Tel: 905 891 8412
Tradition: Theravada

White Wind Zen Community
240 Daly Avenue, Ottawa, ON K1N 6G2
Tel: 613 562 1568
Tradition: Zen

Zen Buddhist Temple
86 Vaughan Road, Toronto, ON M6C 2M1
Tel: 416 658 0137
Tradition: Zen

Zen Center of Vancouver
4269 Brant street, Vancouver, BC V5N 5B5
Tel: 604 879 0229
Tradition: Zen

France
Centre Bouddhique International
7 Firmin Bourgeois, 93350 Le Bourget
Tel: 01 48 35 22 49
Tradition: Theravada

Centre de la Falaise Verte
La Riaille, 07800 Saint Laurent de Pape
Tel: 04 75 85 10 39
Tradition: Zen

Centre d'Etudes de Chanteloupe
La Bicanderie, 24290 Saint-Leon-sur-Vezere
Tel: 05 53 50 75 24
Tradition: Tibetan

Dana
22 Avenue Pasteur, 93100 Montreuil
Tel: 01 49 88 91 65
Tradition: Zen

Dojo Zen de Paris
175 Rue Tolbiac, 75013 Paris
Tel: 01 53 80 19 19
Tradition: Zen

Institut Ganden Ling
Chemin de la Passerelle,
77250 Veneux-les-Sablons
Tel: 01 64 31 14 82
Tradition: Tibetan

Institut Karma Ling
Hameau de Saint-Hugon, 07310 Arvillard
Tel: 04 79 25 78 00
Tradition: Tibetan

Monastere Bodhinyanarama
6 Chemin de Boucharin, 07300 Tournon
Tel: 04 75 08 86 69
Tradition: Theravada

Plum Village
Meyrac, Loubes-Bernac, 47120 Duras
Tel: 05 53 94 75 40
Tradition: Zen (Thich Nhat Hanh)

Vipassana Dhamma Mahi
Le Bois-Plante, 89350 Louesme
Tel: 03 86 45 75 14
Tradition: Theravada

Germany
Aryatara Institut
Barer Str. 70 Rgb, 80799 München
Tel: 089 2781 7227
Tradition: Tibetan

Buddha-Haus
Uttenbuhl 5, D–87466 Oy-Mittelberg
Tel: 08376 502
Tradition: Theravada

Han-Ma-Um Seon Zentrum
Broicherdorfstr, 102, 41564 Kaarst
Tel: 02131 96 9551
Tradition: Zen

Haus der Stille
Muhlenweg 20, D–21514 Roseburg
Tel: 04158 214
Tradition: Theravada

Kamalashila Institut
Schloß Wachendorf, 53894 Mechernich
Tel: 02256 850
Tradition: Tibetan

Seminarhaus Engl
Engle 1, D–84339 Unterdietfurt
Tel: 08728 616
Tradition: Theravada

Tibetische Zentrum
Hermann-Balk-Str. 106, 22147 Hamburg
Tel: 040 6443585
Tradition: Tibetan

Zen-Gemeinschaft Jikishin-Kai
Adalbertstrasse 108, 80798 München
Tel: 089 2719024
Tradition: Zen

Zen Zentrum Berlin
Gottschedstrasse 4, 13357 Berlin
Tel: 030 4654793
Tradition: Zen

Italy
Associazone per la Meditazione
di Consapevolezza
Via Valle di Riva 1, 00141 Roma
Tel: 06 8120138
Tradition: Theravada

Communita Dzogchen Merigar
Arcidossolo, 58031 Grosseto
Tel: 0564 966837
Tradition: Tibetan

Istituto Lama Tzong Khapa
via Poggiberna, 56040 Pomaia
Tel: 050 685654
Tradition: Tibetan

Santacittarama
loc. Brulla, 02030 Frasso Sabino
Tel: 0765 872186
Tradition: Theravada

Scaramuccia – Luogo di Pratica Buddhista
della scuola Linci di Chan
Scaramuccia, 05019 Orvieto Scalo
Tel: 0763 25054
Tradition: Zen

Shobozan Fudenji – Tempio Zen Soto Centro
di studi e Meditazione Buddhista
Bargone 113, 43039 Salsomaggiore
Tel: 0524 565667
Tradition: Zen

New Zealand
Amitabha Hospice Service
PO Box 37, Albany Village, Auckland
Tel: 09 413 9432
Tradition: Tibetan

Bodhinyanarama Forest Monastery
17 Rakau Grove, Stokes Valley, Wellington
Tel: 04 563 7193
Tradition: Theravada

Jam Tse Dhargyä Ling
Dhargyey Buddhist Centre of Love
and Compassion
220 Pipiwai Road, ROAD 6, Whangarei
Tel: 09 435 4113
Tradition: Tibetan

Karma Kagyu Thigsum Chokhorling
Tibetan Buddhist Monastery
66 Bodhisattva Road, ROAD 1,
Kaukapakapa 1250
Tel: 09 420 5428
Tradition: Tibetan

Te Moata Retreat Centre
PO Box 100, Tairua, Coromandel
Tel: 07 868 8798
Tradition: Non-denominational

Zen Society of New Zealand
PO Box 18, 175 Glen Innes, Auckland
Tel: 09 521 1571
Tradition: Zen

Zen Wellington
11 Wesley Road, Wellington
Tel: 09 471 0203
Tradition: Zen

South Africa
The Buddhist Retreat Centre
PO Box 131, Ixopo, Natal 3276
Tel: 0336 341863
Tradition: Non-denominational

Johannesburg Samye Dzong
43 Floss Street, Kensington, 2094
Tel: 011 614 1948
Tradition: Tibetan

Poep Kwang Sa Darma Centre
26 White Street, Robertson, Cape 6705
Tel: 02351 3515
Tradition: Zen

Spain
Centro Budista de Valencia
Plaza rojas Clemente 3bajo, 46008 Valencia
Tel: 392 55 84
Tradition: Western Buddhist

Jiko An – Comunidad Religiosa Zen
del Camino Abierto
Cortigo el Alamillo, 18460 Yegen
Tel: 958 343 185
Tradition: Zen

Nagarjuna C.E.T. Valencia
Calle Joaquin Costa 10, Pta 9, 46005 Valencia
Tel: 6 395 1008
Tradition: Tibetan

O.sel.ling Centro de Retiros
Apartado 99, 18400 Orgiva, Granada
Tel: 58 343 134
Tradition: Tibetan

Templo Luz serena
Banshozan Wakozenji, 46356 Casas del Rio
Tel: 96 230 1055
Tradition: Zen

Switzerland
Buddhistisches Zentrum Zollikon
(YigaA Tschoezin/Rige Tschampa Tschoeling)
Hinterzünen 8
8702 Zollikon

Tel: 01 391 81 66
Tradition: Tibetan

Dhammapala Buddhistisches Kloster
Am Waldrand, CH 3718 Kandersteg
Tel: 033 752 100
Tradition: Theravada

Dojo Zen de Genève
Avenue Calas 16, 1205 Genève
Tel: 022 789 32 93
Tradition: Zen

Meditation Center Beatenberg
Waldegg, CH–3803 Beatenberg
Tel: 033 841 21 31
Tradition: Theravada

Medidationszentrum Haus Tao
CH–9427, Wolfhaden
Tel: 071 44 41 83
Tradition: Zen (Thich Nhat Hanh)

Rapten Choeling
Centre de Hautes Etudes Tibetaines,
1801 Le Mont Pelerin
Tel: 021 921 36 00
Tradition: Tibetan

UK
Amaravati
St Margaret's Lane, Great Gaddesden,
Hemel Hempstead HP1 3DZ
Tel: 01442 843411
Tradition: Theravada

Birmingham Buddhist Vihara
47 Carlyle Road, Edgbaston,
Birmingham B16 9BH
Tel: 0121 454 2782
Tradition: Theravada

The Buddhist Society
58 Eccleston Square, London SW1V 1PH
Tel: 0207 834 5858
Tradition: Non-denominational

Gaia House
West Ogwell, Newton Abbott,
Devon TQ12 6EN
Tel: 01626 333613
Tradition: Non-denominational

Jamyang Buddhist Centre
The Old Courthouse, 43 Renfrew Road,
Kennington, London SE11 4NA
Tel: 0207 820 8787
Tradition: Tibetan

Kagyu Samye Ling Monastery & Tibetan Centre
Eskdalemuir, Langholm,
Dumfriesshire DG13 0QL
Tel: 01387 373232
Tradition: Tibetan

Lam Rim Bristol Buddhist Centre
12 Victoria Place, Bedminster,
Bristol BS3 3BP
Tel: 0117 963 9089/923 1138
Tradition: Tibetan

London Buddhist Vihara
Dharmapala Building, The Avenue,
London W4 1UD
Tel: 0208 995 9493
Tradition: Theravada

Throssel Hole Buddhist Abbey
Carrshield, Hexham, Northumberland NE47 8AL
Tel: 01434 345 204
Tradition: Zen

Western Ch'an Fellowship
Secretary, Simon Child, 24 Woodgate Ave,
Bury, Lancs BL9 7RU
Tel: 0161 761 1945
Tradition: Zen

Yonhwasa
5 Waters Road, Kingston upon Thames,
Surrey KT1 3LW
Tel: 0208 549 6092
Tradition: Zen

USA

Bay Zen Center
5600 Snake Road, Oakland, CA 94611
Tel: 510 482 2533
Tradition: Zen

Bhavana Society
Rt. 1, Box 218–3, High View, WV 26808
Tel: 304 856 3241
Tradition: Theravada

Buddhist Peace Fellowship
PO Box 4650, Berkeley, CA 94704
Tel: 510 525 8596
Tradition: Non-denominational

Cambridge Insight Meditation Center
331 Broadway, Cambridge, MA 02138
Tel: 617 491 5070
Tradition: Theravada

Ch'an Meditation Center,
Institute of Chung-Hwa Buddhist Culture
90–56 Corona Avenue, Elmhurst, Queens,
New York, NY 11373
Tel: 718 592 6593
Tradition: Zen

Dzogchen Foundation
PO Box 400734, Cambridge, MA 02140
Tel: 617 628 1702
Tradition: Tibetan

Foundation for the Preservation
of the Mahayana Tradition

International Office, 125B La Posta Road, Tao.,
NM 87571
Tel: 505 758 7766
Tradition: Tibetan

Insight Meditation Society
1230 Pleasant Street, Barre, MA 01005
Tel: 508 355 4378
Tradition: Theravada

Kadampa Center
7404–G Chapel Hill Road, Raleigh, NC 27607
Tel: 919 859 3433
Tradition: Tibetan

Kanzeon Zen Center Utah
1280 East South Temple,
Salt Lake City, UT 84102
Tel: 801 328 8414
Tradition: Zen

Kurukulla Center
PO Box 381202, Cambridge, MA 02238–1202
Tel: 617 624 0177
Tradition: Tibetan

Minnesota Zen Meditation Center
3343 East Calhoun Parkway,
Minneapolis, MN 55408
Tel: 612 822 5313
Tradition: Zen

New York Insight Meditation Center
PO Box 1790, Murray Hill Station, NY 10156
Tel: 917 441 0915
Tradition: Theravada

Ordinary Mind Zendo
33 Greenwich Avenue #4A,
New York, NY 10014
Tel: 212 691 0819
Tradition: Zen

Providence Zen Center
Diamond Hill Zen Monastery,
99 Pond Road, Cumberland, RI 02864–2726
Tel: 401 658 1464
Tradition: Zen

Sakya Monastery of Tibetan Buddhism
108 NW 83rd Street, Seattle, WA 98109
Tel: 206 789 2573
Tradition: Tibetan

San Francisco Zen Center
300 Page Street, San Francisco, CA 94102
Tel: 415 863 3136
Tradition: Zen

Shasta Abbey
3724 Summit Drive, Mount Shasta,
CA 96067–9102
Tel: 530 926 4208
Tradition: Zen

Spirit Rock Meditation Center
PO Box 909, 5000 Sir Francis Drake Blvd,
Woodacre, CA 94973
Tel: 415 488 0164
Tradition: Theravada

Springwater Center
7179 Mill Street, Springwater, NY 14560
Tel: 716 669 2141
Tradition: Non-denominational

Tara Mandala
PO Box 3040, 157 Hot Springs Blvd,
Pagosa Springs, CO 81147
Tel: 970 264 6177
Tradition: Tibetan

Vajrapani Institute
PO Box 2130, Boulder Creek, CA 95006
Tel: 408 338 6654
Tradition: Tibetan

Village Zendo
15 Washington Place, 4E, New York,
NY 10003
Tel: 212 674 0832
Tradition: Zen

Zen Buddhist Temple (Ann Arbor)
1214 Packard Road, Ann Arbor, MI 48104
Tel: 734 761 6520
Tradition: Zen

Zen Center of Los Angeles
923 S. Normandie Ave, Los Angeles,
CA 90006–1301
Tel: 213 387 2351
Tradition: Zen

Zen Center of New York City
500 State Street, Brooklyn, NY 11217
Tel: 212 642 1591
Tradition: Zen

Zen Community of New York
14 Ashburton Place, Yonkers, NY 10703
Tel: 914 376 3900
Tradition: Zen

Zen Community of Oregon
PO Box 7, Corbett, OR 97019
Tel: 503 282 7879
Tradition: Zen

Zen Mountain Monastery
PO Box 197, Mt. Tremper, NY 12457
Tel: 845 688 2228
Tradition: Zen

index

author's acknowledgments

I would like to thank everyone at Frances Lincoln. It has been a pleasure to work with such a professional and attentive team. I am especially grateful to Fiona Robertson, my editor; Cathy Fischgrund, who commissioned the book; and the designers, Becky Clarke and Sarah Slack, who have done a wonderful job. I would like to express my gratitude to Roger Ash Wheeler and Camilla Armstrong, the models for the meditation positions, for their graciousness and poise. In general, I would like to thank everyone I have encountered and learned from. A special thanks to the people who have sat on retreats and helped me with their questions, challenges and dedication, and to everyone in Korea and at the Barn, Sharpham and Gaia House who has made me reflect and ponder. I am indebted to Dr Seri Phongphit's book *Religion in a Changing Society* for many inspiring examples. I have likewise been inspired by the BASE project of the Buddhist Peace Fellowship. And finally it has been a great pleasure to work with Stephen on this book, and to have his photographs included in it.

We hope you enjoyed this title
from Echo Point Books & Media

Before Closing this Book, Two Good Things to Know

Buy Direct & Save

Go to www.echopointbooks.com (click "Our Titles" at top or click "For Echo Point Publishing" in the middle) to see our complete list of titles. We publish books on a wide variety of topics—from spirituality to auto repair.

Buy direct and save 10% at www.echopointbooks.com

DISCOUNT CODE: EPBUYER

Make Literary History and Earn $100 Plus Other Goodies Simply for Your Book Recommendation!

At Echo Point Books & Media we specialize in republishing out-of-print books that are united by one essential ingredient: high quality. Do you know of any great books that are no longer actively published? If so, please let us know. If we end up publishing your recommendation, you'll be adding a wee bit to literary culture and a bunch to our publishing efforts.

Here is how we will thank you:

- A free copy of the new version of your beloved book that includes acknowledgement of your skill as a sharp book scout.
- A free copy of another Echo Point title you like from echopointbooks.com.
- And, oh yes, we'll also send you a check for $100.

Since we publish an eclectic list of titles, we're interested in a wide range of books. So please don't be shy if you have obscure tastes or like books with a practical focus. To get a sense of what kind of books we publish, visit us at www.echopointbooks.com.

If you have a book that you think will work for us,
send us an email at editorial@echopointbooks.com

CPSIA information can be obtained
at www.ICGtesting.com
Printed in the USA
LVHW071123270122
709436LV00010B/307